INSIDER'S GUIDE TO SECURITY CLEARANCES

Get the Clearance and Land the Job

By Jeffrey W. Bennett

ISP, SAPPC, SFPC, ISOC

Red Bike Publishing

INSIDER'S GUIDE TO SECURITY CLEARANCES

Get the Clearance and Land the Job

By Jeffrey W. Bennett

ISP, SAPPC, SFPC, ISOC

RED BIKE PUBLISHING

If you want more information about security clearances, check out our video.
http://www.redbikepublishing.com/security/

Praise for Other Red Bike Publishing Books

DoD Security Clearance and Contractors Guidebook

"Informative book for people who are new and/or experienced In Industrial Security." Amazon.com Book Review

"An excellent book for companies trying to get into the world of classified government contracts. It is a great starting point for new Facility Security Officers, telling them what they need to know in order to be successful at their job." Amazon.com Book Review

ISP Certification-The Industrial Security Professional Exam Manual

"Written by a security consultant with twenty-two years of experience in military intelligence, contracting and security, ISP Certification: The Industrial Security Professional Exam Manual is an instructional resource created to provide career security specialists with what they need to know to protect our nation's secrets. The text offers practical advice for security professionals and a working understanding of the NISPOM and Presidential Executive Orders implementing the National Industrial Security Program, but the heart of ISP Certification is its four practice tests designed to probe the depths of one's knowledge. An absolute "must-have" for anyone in federal positions requiring a thorough knowledge of security procedures, and highly recommended for the libraries of federal agencies." Midwest Book Review

"Right on target! Jeffrey Bennett's exam manual is the perfect supplement to the NISPOM for anyone preparing to take the Industrial Security Professional certification exam. The approach is clear and easy to use. It's definitely worth the price and more." William H. Henderson, author, Security Clearance Manual

"You have captivated the reader's interest!! Throughout the reading, you continue to address educational encouragement, experience and networking. All of which are mandatory in taking the ISP exam. The emphasis on mentoring just goes to show you how important it is to have support of your peers. Many who may be apprehensive about taking the exam, probably feel like they are all alone and no one is there to lean on. This book is an amazing tool to help guide and support those interested in rising to the next level. This book supports the certification's demonstration of willingness for self-improvement and dedication to the profession. Thank you for assisting me in reaching my full potential and there is no doubt in my mind as to where I am headed."Deb Jaramillo, ASIS North AL Chapter Secretary

"As a seasoned security professional, I found the Industrial Security Professional Exam Manual to be very clear, brief and concise. The ISP manual is a must read for anyone anticipating taking the ISP exam. Whether you are a seasoned security professional or a newbie to the world of security, this book is a keeper. Thank you for putting out such a Great Book ."Diane Griffin, President/CEO, Security First & Associates LLC

"Like many seasoned industrial security representatives, I feel like I know it all. I have been in this industry almost 25 years; I know where to look for answers, and I have my contacts. But one day it occurred to me just how much has changed during my career - enter the Internet, enter computer based training, enter instant security clearances (Interims), enter the JPAS/e-QIP interface, enter diminished contact with my cleared employees and visitors. Admitting that the contact with my cleared employees is not as intimate as it used to have to be, somehow I felt that I was losing touch with my own skill set because of it. Jeffrey Bennett's book is very insightful into our industry, for he works with and supports, and motivates, this industry. You should consider buying the ISP Certification - The Industrial Security Professional Exam Manual, and spend 30 minutes with it each evening after work. Reinvigorate yourself. Give your imagination and professional growth some quiet stimulation. Remember. Refresh yourself. The best security education dollar you can spend, and not even leave home."Lisa Doman, Sierra Vista, AZ

"I am impressed with his knowledge base of our field and he has been helpful when called upon. I purchased ISP Exam Manual. The set up and information contained in the book has increased my confidence in taking the exam." TJ Knight, FSO, Applied Geo Technologies, Huntsville, AL

"Jeff provides a paramount service with his book that assists in taking the ISP test. He gives insight into what is needed to help you be certified in the security industry today. Jeff's dedication and attention to detail is second to none and I highly recommend him on a professional level."Kenneth Wontz, President. Trinity Security Consultants, VA

"As a retired US Army, Chief Warrant Officer Five (CW5), Counteringelligence Officer; former Special Agent, Defense Investigative Service (DIS); former Special Agent Defense Security Service (DSS); former US Army Liaison Officer to Headquarters, Department of Defense (DoD), Alexandria, VA, Counterintelligence Division for Counterintelligence Issues, and former owner of a Small Veteran's Business, under a DoD contract to conduct Background Investigations for DoD Personnel Security Clearances, I consider this book to be brief and it makes the complex simple. This ISP Manual is a must for those preparing to take the ISP Certification Exam."

"I bought this book 8 months prior to taking the exam, and coupled with the modules on the NCMS website, passed my exam on the first try. Most of us are not using all the skill sets of an industrial security professional but only the ones necessary to perform our jobs, this book takes the reader to other areas previously unexplored. If you are studying for the ISP exam, I highly recommend this book."

National Industrial Security Program Operating Manual (NISPOM)

"Long gone is my big and bulky 3 ring binder. This book (NISPOM) takes up a fraction of the room on your desk, and is portable enough to take to any security meeting." Amazon.com Book Review

ABOUT THE AUTHOR

Jeffrey W. Bennett, ISP SFPC, SAPPC, ISOC, is experienced in Security and Cyber-Security with the U.S. Army, as a Defense Contractor, and as a Facility Security Officer (FSO). He believes that integrity, influence and credibility are paramount qualities required of security professionals. His primary goal is to show security specialists how to bring about security awareness, build influence within the organization and to make a difference where they work.

Jeff advises on national security issues and is a former Army officer who has served in military intelligence, logistics and speaks three languages. He has an MBA from Columbia College and a Masters Degree in Acquisitions and Procurement Management from Webster University. A teacher at heart, he is board certified to protect classified information. He speaks, writes and provides products to help professionals better protect sensitive and classified information.

As a niche leader, Jeffrey W. Bennett has written and published many niche books with his company Red Bike Publishing. To find out more about him, visit: www.redbikepublishing.com

ABOUT RED BIKE PUBLISHING...

Mission:

Red Bike Publishing exists to create value for our partners, shareholders, and customers by building a business to last.

As the preeminent niche publishing organization, we offer what other publishers cannot: focused delivery of industry publications to enhance the professional's skill level. We do this by writing and publishing superior nonfiction, traditional, and eBooks, and by providing empowering training resources at affordable prices.

Vision:

Red Bike Publishing will be valued for our one-of-a-kind niche publishing and the ability to positively impact our customers.

See more at _www.redbikepublishing.com_

Acknowledgement

None of this would have been possible without the love and support of my family, friends and professionals I have met along the way.

I would like to thank Shama Patel for her social media support and editing services. You can reach her at Evening Light Designs, LLC https://www.eveninglightdesigns.com

CONTENTS

FOREWORD

I wrote this book after many years of teaching security managers how to protect classified information. I developed a good relationship with the cleared employees whose job it was to develop security programs to protect classified information. Soon I began to appear on talk radio shows, blogs, and articles that began to reach a broad audience. This broader audience included people who wanted to get security clearances. As my exposure grew, so did my understanding of just how strong the rumors about security clearances were and how much information the general population lacked.

Opportunities abound in the defense industry where nearly every job description requires a security clearance to perform on the contracts.

Classified contracts require services that include staffing, janitorial, graphic design, accounting, finance and more. Technical experience is needed as well with mechanics, software designers, engineers, program managers and their supporting staff requiring these clearances.

For the unfamiliar, the security clearance process may seem daunting. The lack of information of how to get started, the required forms, interviews, waiting, and expectations can make the entire experience out of the individual's control. However, there is a well-established and efficient process that the government undertakes and you can be in as much control of the experience as possible with just a little coaching from this book.

It is my hope to provide information that will inform the general public, assist employees with the security clearance process, and ease the application process.

You may be reading this book either in college, gainfully employed outside of the defense industry, or starting a business, and may be interested in gaining a security clearance and starting a career. There are more than 13,000 Cleared Defense Contractors (CDC) making up the industrial base. Though you may be aware of the opportunities, you may be wondering how to get started and I usually get asked the following question:

"How do I get a clearance so I can get a classified job?"

It's a great question, but it can't be answered easily as asked. The clearance comes after the job requirements. The question is often asked and in the form asked, skips right by the most fundamental question of whether or not an individual qualifies for a clearance and what is the process for getting a clearance. I will attempt to answer the first question by providing answers to the other two questions:

Can I get a security clearance?

Yes, the security clearance process is open to U.S. Citizens. If after a thorough investigation you are deemed trustworthy, you may be granted a question. However, not just anyone can apply; see the next question.

How do I get the security Clearance?

By applying for a job that requires a security clearance or starting your own company and winning classified contracts.

One final very popular question or grand finale if you will: How long does it take to get a security clearance?

This could take a few months to over a year depending on the investigation and adjudication of findings. The investigation is very in depth and depends a lot on information the applicant provides on the SF-86 application. We will discuss more in detail later, but to give you perspective, search SF-86 online and review the questions. You can reduce the time it takes to get your clearance by researching answers, compiling them for quick response, or even filling out the form and keeping a copy with back up documentation on your computer.

Once you apply for the clearance process, you can access the information and fill out the application easily. If you wait until the day you apply, it could take weeks to get prepared. BE CAREFUL, the information you collect on yourself and family members is very sensitive, so PROTECT it.

This book will discuss the answers to these questions in depth in the following chapters.

SOME BACKGROUND

My Experience

I felt the need to write this background information to help you better understand, through my personal experience, how to use your skills experiences to get that desired security clearance job. Whether you want to join a Cleared Defense Contractor (CDC) as a cleared employee or start your own CDC, my experience might help.

I got my first security clearance after joining the Army. My job required it, so the recruiter assisted me in filling out the required security clearance investigation request forms. Looking back, I feel sorry that he had to work so hard in filling out the forms. He spent many evenings at my parents' home going through records to complete the forms. We had to go through address books, school records, phone books and more. This was before computers, so the search was daunting and took a long time.

What I want you to get from this story is that the paperwork did not take long, but the research did. There are things you can do right now to shorten the process before you even get started.

I maintained a security clearance from the day it was granted. Every job both while serving and after I got out have required a security clearance. The beautiful thing is once you receive the security clearance, it is transferrable between agencies and jobs. You can continue to use it as long as you are performing on jobs requiring the clearance and you continue to demonstrate trustworthiness. Trustworthiness is continuously evaluated as long as you have a clearance and clearance investigations are conducted periodically depending on security clearance level.

Once I left the Army I picked up a security clearance job that required my job skills. At first I worked in the security industry developing security programs to protect classified information. This encompassed many tasks that helped me get started in my consulting business. I handled security clearances, classified information, and the storage and disposition of all things involved in classified contracts.

Red Bike Publishing.

My company Red Bike Publishing is registered as a defense contractor. After many years protecting classified information, I decided to teach the skill. My first book endeavor was a product to teach other security professionals how to study for security certification exam and maximize their chances of passing. I began providing the coaching and material called, ISP Certification-The Industrial Security Professional Exam Manual.

Soon I began to write and publish books discussing how to protect classified information once a defense contractor wins a classified contract. As I discovered in my profession, there is a teachable system in place and a gap for the books and training. The books and training are applicable to the cleared employee population and useful in training the security manager responsible for developing the security program to protect classified information. If you are interested in finding more information, the following books and training are available at _https://www.redbikepublishing.com_.

We Print Government Documents:

National Industrial Security Program Operating Manual (NISPOM) – This is the Department of Defense guidebook on how CDCs should employ cleared contractors and protect classified information.

The Self-Inspection Handbook for NISP Contractors – This is a government publication of how a CDC can self-evaluate its application of NISPOM. It should be referred to regularly and can assist with the government security audit and review requirements.

International Traffic in Arms Regulation (ITAR) – This is the Department of State product of how to protect export-controlled technology.

We Write Original Books

How to Win U.S. Government Contracts and Classified Work – Teaches how to prepare for and bid on classified contracts. It includes how to initiate security clearance requests and train the cleared employee work force to perform on and protect classified work.

We Developed Training:

Initial Security Awareness Training – Required training topics for all cleared employees that can be downloaded and presented

Insider Threat Training - This training program includes the NISPOM identified Insider Threat Training requirements.

Security Agreement Briefing - Newly cleared employees must sign an SF-312, Non Disclosure Agreement. This is the agreement briefing and preliminary training.

Derivative Classifier Training - This training can help cleared contractors ensure that all personnel who perform duties as derivative classifiers meet the training requirements.

Your Start

Now that I shared my experience, hopefully it will provide ideas for you to begin your security cleared future. Ask yourself the following questions concerning security clearance jobs.

What is lacking in the industry?

How can I help?

Which CDCs or government agencies are hiring employees with my skills?

Could I start my own business and become a CDC using my skills?

Finding answers to these questions should stir up some momentum. There are job finders on the internet where you can join for free, post your resume and apply for clearance jobs without even having a security clearance. Professional job finders and recruiters are available as well. I recommend starting with clearancejobs.com and usajobs.com as the most reputable.

The search takes time, so have a backup plan. If you don't have a job yet, don't wait for that clearance job. Some employees may go right past a resume where it is evident the employee does not have a clearance. Smaller CDCs cannot afford to wait the 6 months to a year it takes to get notification back on a security clearance. However, larger companies may be more apt to take on employees and give them temporary fork while they wait for the clearance.

If you desire the clearance job and do not have a clearance, go ahead and apply, but stay in your current situation and wait for the opportunity. In the meantime, start getting your information together so that you can easily fill out the required paperwork. We will discuss those steps later.

A note to Entrepreneurs

This book is also for those of you with an entrepreneurial spirit. You see a problem and offer a solution that is accurate, to the point, and both affordable and valuable to a government or CDC consumer. Your passion for your subject motivates you to work beyond what you normally might give to an employer, and your priorities have shifted somewhat to accommodate this desire.

Entrepreneurs are often known for great ability to overcome incredible odds to provide real solutions. Entrepreneurs are celebrated media and industry. The defense industry also values this spirit. Consider problems facing the defense industry and solutions you have. You may have the desired skills that a government organization or CDC may want to sponsor.

Summary

This introduction has focused on how one can get a security clearance and how to apply for security clearance work. The process depends on a classified contract need as well as the qualification of the person applying for the classified work. Your part is to find the security clearance work and demonstrate you have the skills and qualifications to apply for it. You should also prepare well in advance for filling out the application. Access the internet and review the SF-86 and review the information required. Then gather information about where you have lived, worked, studied, and your financial records.

NOTE TO THE READER

We have written this book after having studied the craft of national security and obtained certifications from both the DoD and professional organizations that demonstrate competency in protecting classified information. This book has been reviewed and edited by some of the most experienced Facility Security Officers and defense contractors in the business. It is reviewed often and revised to keep current.

Those who know how to execute classified contracts are in demand. Additionally, the Departments of Defense, Department of Energy, the Nuclear Regulatory Commission, Central Intelligence Agency and their many supporting contractors are in great need of experienced and qualified cleared employees. As the industry becomes more demanding and positions more competitive, today's cleared employees need to be competitive.

This book is designed to give the unfamiliar general public a glimpse into the National Industrial Security Program. Our intention is to help you understand what is required of you to become cleared employees and working on classified contracts. Any security clearance and compliance related problems and issues that you may face during the process should be pursued with the Cognizant Security Agency (CSA), Government Contracting Activity (GCA) or other Federal agencies and legal activities.

This book addresses both Cleared Defense Contractors (CDC) and cleared employees. By way of clarification, CDCs are the organizations or businesses that have been awarded security clearances based on classified contracts and the cleared employees are the employees working on the classified contracts; we'll explain more later.

 Not every CDC is the same and classified contracts further differentiate requirements. Each CDC and cleared employee may have a unique mission based on skill sets and core competencies. Each contract has unique requirements based on product and service needs. Defense contractors working on classified contracts will have further defined roles based on requirements listed in the Contract Security Classification Specification (DD Form 254) and contract clauses and language. Specifically, cleared contractors have unique security requirements based on the contract identifying the clearance level and classified storage level.

Defense contractors who desire to perform on classified contracts do not always know where to go to find information on how to get a security clearance and what might be expected of them. Some might become CDCs after they purposefully bid for classified contracts while others find that contracts beginning as unclassified may become classified at a later time, leaving them with a steep learning curve. The leadership of companies not experienced in working with classified contracts may not know where to look for information or gain access to training or possible expenses until after the Government grants their facility and personnel security clearances.

A National Level View of Protecting the Nation's Secrets

As a short explanation of why things are classified, we will explain the National Industrial Security Program (NISP). Under the NISP, the Department of Defense, Department of Energy, Director of National Intelligence, the Nuclear Regulatory Commission and their cleared con- tractors are charged with protecting classified information. Classified information is US Government material, documents, software, hardware, or any other official information in any other format that requires protection from unauthorized disclosure. Unauthorized disclosure could cause damage to national security. Cleared Defense Contractors and cleared employees have demonstrated the ability to be entrusted with government owned classified information.

Each of the above-mentioned government agencies are also known as Cognizant Security Agencies (CSA) and each has established guidelines for protecting classified information and ensuring compliance. Though each agency has its own written guidelines, the NISP ensures that each follows a national standard. The CSAs have Cognizant Security Offices (CSO) that take care of administrative functions.

This book addresses how to get the security clearance and touches a little on the responsibility to protect classified information in the Department of Defense (DoD) and their contractors. The DoD is a CSA and Defense Counterintelligence and Security Agency (DCSA) is the CSO. Guidelines for protecting classified information in the DoD are found in the National Industrial Security Program Operating Manual

(NISPOM). The NISPOM provides oversight and inspection guidelines to the CDC to ensure classified information is not disclosed in an unauthorized manner. The loss, compromise or suspected compromise of classified information should be investigated and reported. Loss, compromise or suspected compromise could occur without proper control, accountability, and documentation of classified information.

If this sounds like something you want to pursue as a career goal, please read further.

WHO THIS BOOK IS FOR

The Opportunity

There are many security clearance jobs available right now. It's easy to qualify and if you have the right skills, you can go to work right away. Perhaps you are one of the many who have questions about getting a security clearance.

The Problem

Maybe you are interested either as an employee or business owner in getting a security clearance, but don't know how to get started.

There are numerous training opportunities within the industrial security community, government services, and professional organizations. However, other than government regulations, there are few published books addressing the subject.

Employees and defense contractors who desire to have a security clearance are often uninformed on how to get them. Some think that security clearances can be granted to allow them to be more employable. Businesses may want to have a security clearance for their businesses so they can get more work. However, security clearances are granted based on a contract and legitimate government work that requires access to classified information.

THE SOLUTION

This book is intended to provide answers that help those who would like to know more about what it takes to get a clearance or prepare for work on classified contracts. It will assist the college student studying industrial security or homeland security, upstart companies looking for work, and new industrial security employees with understanding the fundamental demands of a career in Industrial Security.

This eBook is written with you in mind and is addressed specifically for defense contractors operating under the Department of Defense guidance. Other Government agencies may have different procedures. However, this book can be used as a general reference regardless of which agency the contractor is operating under. This book reflects requirements as found in the National Industrial Security Program Operating Manual (NISPOM)

This eBook is divided into chapters rich with information on the steps necessary and coaching tips on how to get a security clearance. The way our book differs from other security clearance books resides in following chapters describing what to do once a clearance is granted. This is an overall view that is covered in more detail in the National Industrial Security Program Operating Manual (NISPOM) and the book, DOD Security Clearances and Contracts Guidebook both available from Red Bike Publishing.

The chapters walk the reader along the process of registering as a defense contractor, the facility security clearance process, the personnel security clearance process, the required appointed positions, the National Industrial Security Program and how to protect classified information. For example, once a facility clearance is granted, a Facility Security Officer (FSO) must be appointed to manage the security of classified information and contracts. This book addresses the FSO duties that may be assumed by the business owner or an appointed cleared employee. It also lets the non-business owner reader know what to expect once they get their security clearance.

Perhaps you are one of the many readers who have questions about getting a security clearance. Maybe you are interested either as an employee or business owner in getting a security clearance, but don't know how to get started. This book is written with you in mind and is addressed specifically for defense contractors operating under the Department of Defense (DoD) guidance. This book reflects requirements as found in the National Industrial Security Program Operating Manual (NISPOM) and other Government agencies have their own guidelines. However, this book can be used as a general reference regardless of which agency the contractor is operating under.

This book is intended to provide answers that help those who would like to know more about what it takes to get a clearance or prepare for work on classified contracts. It will assist the college student studying industrial security or homeland security, upstart companies looking for work, and new cleared employees with understanding the fundamental demands of working on classified contracts and a career in the defense industry.

This book is divided into chapters with that information in mind. The way our book differs from other security clearance books resides in following chapters describing what to do once a clearance is granted. We can't promise to help you get a clearance. Getting a security clearance depends on whether or not you or your business are trustworthy and you have products or services needed by the government or another contractor. This book only provides an overall view that is covered in more detail in the *National Industrial Security Program Operating Manual (NISPOM)* and the book, *Security Clearances and Performing on Classified Contracts* both available from Red Bike Publishing.

The chapters walk the reader along the requirement of registering as a defense contractor, the facility security clearance and personnel security clearance process, the required appointed positions, and how to protect classified information once the clearances are granted. For example, once a facility clearance is granted, a Facility Security Officer (FSO) must be appointed to manage the security of classified information and contracts. This book addresses some high level FSO duties that may be assumed by the business owner or any other appointed cleared employee.

Finally, this book is intended to provide information about the security clearance process. The author does not guarantee that the reader will get a security clearance. All coordination for the security clearance process should be conducted through the government, Defense Security Services and a Facility Security Officer.

The next few chapters are purposely arrange to narrate the NISP requirements. Each can be read independently, but are provided sequentially. The following chapters are ordered accordingly:

Why Security Clearances: This chapter describes the need for security clearances and why and how information is classified.

The Facility security Clearance (FCL): This chapter describes how to obtain the FCL. The organization is required to have a security clearance to perform on classified contracts. The FCL is awarded first, then the employees. This chapter applies to entrepreneurs or others who want to establish their organizations as cleared defense contractors.

The Personnel security Clearance (PCL): This chapter describes how to apply for an employee security clearance and how they are awarded. It is appropriate for those who wish to pursue jobs that require security clearances.

After the Security Clearance: This chapter describes what happens after the FCL and PCLs are awarded.

WHY SECURITY CLEARANCES

A NATIONAL LEVEL VIEW OF PROTECTING THE NATION'S SECRETS

Under the National Industrial Security Program (NISP), the Department of Defense, Department of Energy, Director of National Intelligence, the Nuclear Regulatory Commission and their cleared contractors are charged with protecting classified information. Classified information is material, documents, software, hardware, or any other official government information in any other format that requires protection from unauthorized disclosure. Such disclosure could cause varying degrees of damage to national security depending on the classification level.

Those who share the perception that civilians should not be able to access classified information should be confident in the actual governance involved. In fact, the government determines the classification level, and after signed agreements, provides the required classified information to the contractors. The Cleared Defense Contractor (CDC) agrees to protect the classified information and follows the required guidance. For the Department of Defense (DoD), this guidance is provided in the National Industrial Security Program Operating Manual (NISPOM).

The NISPOM is applicable to both CDC and cleared employees. As earlier stated, CDCs are the organizations or businesses with security clearances and the cleared employees are the employees working on the classified contracts.

The NISPOM is provided by the Department of Defense (DoD) to the DoD CDC. The NISPOM is a set of guidelines that the CDC can use to develop and implement their security programs to protect classified information. The CDC can implement the NISPOM to prevent the unauthorized disclosure of classified information. The DoD's Cognizant Security Office (CSO) provides inspections and audits to determine how well the CDC applies the NISPOM.

In cases of security violations, the loss, compromise or suspected compromise of classified information should be investigated and reported. Without this oversight, governance, and agreements, loss, compromise or suspected compromise could occur at a large scale.

How the U.S. Government assigns classification levels

How do classified items receive their designations? Who is responsible for assigning classification levels? What recourse do security managers have after discovering a classification error? Can anything be assigned a classification level by anyone? These are questions that may be asked by those new to the NISP. Although there is guidance to demonstrate proper control, accountability, documentation, storage, dissemination and destruction of classified material, CDCs with newly awarded Facility Clearances (FCL) can benefit from the discussion in this section and in extreme detail as found in *NISPOM* and *DoD Security and Contracts Guidebook.*

Executive Orders

The U.S. President signs the Executive Orders (EO) defining Classified National Security Information. The latest EO defines and delivers a cohesive method for classification designation, protecting and declassifying national security information.

Original Classification Authority (OCA)

The Original Classification Authority (OCA) is the government entity that determines classification levels. They follow a six step process that determines sensitivity, demonstrates the level of damage to national security, and communicates that classification level. The OCA assigns classification to qualifying equipment, documents, tools, pictures, software, and other items that need protection against unauthorized disclosure. For the purposes of this book, we will refer to classified items of all configurations and media as classified information.

The Government has designed policy to ensure that classified material is protected at the level designated to prevent unauthorized disclosure. The President has designated the authority to assign a classification level and the EO defines an accountability process to ensure classification is assigned at the appropriate level and protection is adequate. The person holding the appointed position of OCA has both the duty and responsibility to classify information properly.

Classified information is marked with TOP SECRET, SECRET, or CONFIDENTIAL and must be afforded protection at the appropriate level. TOP SECRET has more restrictions than SECRET and SECRET has more restrictions than CONFIDENTIAL and each must be protected according to the classification markings. The classification levels and definitions are based on damage to national security if unauthorized disclosure occurred:

- TOP SECRET could reasonably be expected to cause exceptionally grave damage to national security
- SECRET could reasonably be expected to cause serious damage;
- CONFIDENTIAL could reasonably be expected cause damage

When the classification level is determined, the OCA places the proper markings. The markings indicate the level of classification, identify the exact information to be protected, provide guidance on downgrading and declassification, give reasons for classification and sources of classification, and warn of special access, control or safeguarding requirements.

To prevent system abuse, EO's provide guidance to train and prevent OCAs from arbitrarily assigned a classification level. The information has to meet certain criteria before the level can be designated. As over-classification results in unnecessary costs, under-classification can lead to possible compromise of classified information. To better prevent unauthorized disclosure and ensure that classification is assigned to only that information requiring protection, the following specifics are provided with examples. In cases where items may be assigned an original classification, four conditions must be met:

- A designated OCA is applying the classification level
- The information is owned by, produced for, or is controlled by the U.S. Government
- Information meets one of eight categories:
  1. Military plans, weapons systems or operations
  2. Foreign government information
  3. Intelligence activities, sources or methods or cryptology
  4. Foreign relations or activities of the United States including

confidential sources

5. Scientific, technological, or economic matters relating to national security, including defense against transnational terrorism
6. U.S. programs for safeguarding nuclear materials or facilities
7. Vulnerabilities of systems, installations, infrastructures, projects, plans or protection services related to national security including terrorism
8. Weapons of mass destruction

Once the OCA determines something is classified, their next step is to designate the classification level based on the degree of damage that unauthorized disclosure could cause to national security to include transnational terrorism. The OCA should be able to easily and effectively communicate damage. This is all done to determine what is classified and how it is to be protected. This is then communicated to CDCs performing work on the contracts that require access to the information deemed classified by the OCA.

National Industrial Security Program (NISP)

The US Government awards contracts, grants and licenses to defense contractors in the course of providing a product or service and these contracts, grants and licenses may be classified in nature. The NISP is designed to protect classified government information that is released to CDCs. The result is a partnership between the government and the cleared contractor and an agreement to protect the classified information at the level the OCA has determined it to be.

The NISP's purpose is to safeguard classified information that has been or may be released to "…current, prospective, or former contractors, licensees, or grantees of United States agencies". It provides guidance for safeguarding classified information, required security education topics and training programs.

The National Industrial Security Program Operating Manual (NISPOM)

Every cleared contractor should have the NISPOM readily available either in print or on their computer. Program managers, engineers, security all cleared employees should also possess it as it is the guide providing guidelines and procedures for preventing unauthorized disclosure of classified material. The NISPOM applies to authorized users of classified information and equips those working on classified contracts with instruction on how to implement the NISP within their organizations. It is up to the CDC and the CSO to work together in providing accurate interpretation of the NISPOM to the specific classified contract requirements. It is this interpretation that the CSO will use while conducting annual security reviews.

The Secretary of Defense and the other government agencies apply the concept of risk management while implementing the NISPOM. There are three factors necessary in determining risk. The first is the damage to national security that could be reasonably expected to result from unauthorized disclosure of classified material. The second factor is the existing or anticipated threat to disclosure of information. The third factor is the short and long term costs of the requirements, restrictions, and other safeguards. The second and third factors aren't spelled out in the NISPOM, but are recognized as legitimate concerns that the FSO and CSO should be prepared to address.

The Facility Security Officer

You might be asking, why all the emphasis on the NISPOM and FSO? Isn't this book about security clearances? Yes it is. It's all about security clearances and FSOs are a large part of the process. Those who are in the process of obtaining an FCL or are currently performing on classified contracts, should be prepared to appoint a cleared employee to perform FSO duties.

Those employees who will be awarded a clearance, should realize that the FSO is on their team to initiate the clearance, answer questions about your clearance and is an integral part in the continuous evaluation process. The FSO is going to make or break your security clearance capability. Security clearances and FSOs go hand in hand; one does not go without the other.

Protection of Classified Information

Access to classified information requires authorization based on a security clearance and need to know of the information. Security clearances are awarded based on favorable information gathered from a properly executed investigation. This process can take over 12 months to complete. After the clearance is granted and prior to gaining access to the classified information, the individual signs a Classified Information Non Disclosure Agreement (SF 312). Cleared employees with access to classified information are trained on proper safeguarding, and sanctions imposed on those who fail to protect it from unauthorized disclosure. Learning how to protect, document and account for classified information will help identify and prevent espionage, theft and other events of unauthorized disclosure.

SUMMARY

The OCA makes classification determinations based on a process. The classification is then provided to the CDC supporting classified contracts. Performance under classified contracts is managed by the government. The government provides the necessary classified information to the CDC and the CDC uses that information to perform their work. Through oversight, checks, and balances the performance of classified work by contractors is a well governed process that limits risk of unauthorized disclosure.

The NISP exists to protect Government classified information at CDCs from unauthorized disclosure. It provides classified national security protection information and delivers a cohesive method for the assignment of a classification, protecting and declassifying national security information. The NISP's guidelines describe the authority to classify information and provides strict requirements. The NISPOM was created to provide guidance on protecting classified information.

FACILITY SECURITY CLEARANCES

Classified information must be protected. Part of the protection is to ensure only properly investigated and vetted cleared employees with need to know get access to classified information.

Defense contractor employees are required to have a personnel security clearance (PCL) and need to know before being granted access to classified information. The PCL is also related to a facility security clearance (FCL) held by the cleared contractor they work for. Respectively, the defense contractors are required to have a FCL prior to performing on classified contracts. What does this mean? It means the cleared contractor and cleared employee has been thoroughly investigated and properly vetted before even being considered eligible to receive classified information.

Not any organization can apply for a security clearance. They must be sponsored by a Prime Contractor or Government Contracting Activity (GCA). The FCLs are granted to defense contractors and PCLs are awarded to their employees only after an investigation and adjudication. Therefore, think of a security clearance as the administrative determination that someone is eligible from a national security basis for access to classified information.

How Defense Contractors Get Facility Security Clearances

A defense contractor is a business entity that has registered to contract with the US Government and has registered with the Central Contractor Registration. A Cleared Defense Contractor (CDC) is the designation of a U.S. Government Contractor facility that has been granted a Facility Clearance, authorizing them to perform on classified contracts. An uncleared defense contractor may bid on a classified contract without possessing an FCL. However, they must be cleared before working on the classified contract.

Many defense contractors may find it difficult to find and compete for classified contracts. They may have a unique skill that is hard to identify contracts requiring those skills. But this should not be a deterrent as uncleared defense contractor may partner with or team with an existing CDC for sponsorship. For example, suppose a major defense contractor is performing on a classified contract for engineering support. Their core competencies provide much needed results but they are in need of a cleared widget maker to make a peripheral piece of hardware. The prime defense contractor is familiar with the excellent work performed by a small uncleared defense contractor. The company does not have a clearance but the cleared prime contractor can award a subcontract and sponsor the winning company for a security clearance.

The Government Contractor Relationship

The figures below demonstrate the relationship between the government and the contractor. The relationship includes the The Government Contracting Agency (GCA) who provides classified work to cleared defense contractors through awarding contracts. The GCA is where the program office, contracts managers, logistics, and contract awarders are located

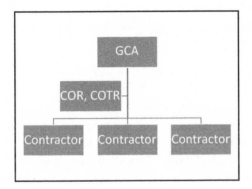

The Contracting Officer's Representative / Contracting Officer's Technical Representative ensures the contract requirements and technical work are delivered as defined in the contract and interact with the contractor.

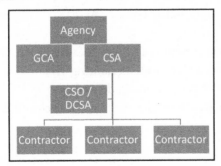

Cognizant Security Agency / Cognizant Security Office oversees protection of the GCA's classified information.

The Facility Security Clearance Process

The following information is specifically related to getting a security clearance to perform on a classified contract. The business should work with the Government Contracting Activity (GCA) and Cognizant Security Agency (CSA) or Organization (CSO). The Defense Counter-intelligence Security Agency (DCSA) is the CSO for the Department of Defense (DoD) and this book will refer the CSO and DCSA interchangeably. The DCSA helps the contractor with the security clearance process.

According to the DCSA website, forms and requirements are available @:

https://www.dcsa.mil/Mission-Centers/Critical-Technology-Protection/Facility-Clearance/Checklist-for-a-New-Facility-Clearance/

The facility clearance is required to be in place prior to the contractor performing on classified work. Once the contract is awarded the government contracting activity (GCA) or prime contractor submits the sponsorship letter to the DCSA, the company can begin the process of applying for the clearance. A contractor has to meet five requirements before it can be processed for an FCL.

- Register as a defense contractor for Contractor and Government Entity Code (CAGE)
- Be Sponsored
- Sign Department of Defense Security Agreement
- Complete a Certificate Pertaining To Foreign Interests
- Provide Organization Credentials
- Identify Key management personnel clearances

Register as a defense contractor

A business entity should register with the System For Award Management (SAM):

https://www.sam.gov/SAM/

SAM assists the government contracting activities with information on defense contractors and registration is required in order to be awarded contracts by the federal government. Once registered, the company will be assigned a Commercial and Government Entity (CAGE) Code. The CAGE code is a form of identification the government assigns to defense contractors. Government agencies use CAGE codes in the course of business with defense contractors. Cleared contractors use the CAGE code to search for classified mailing addresses and conduct business with other cleared contractor companies.

However, registration in no way guarantees that a contract or assistance award will be awarded. Like any business, success is up to the creativity and initiative of the defense contractor.

The following should be performed prior to registering.

Data Universal Numbering System (DUNS) Number provided by Dun and Bradstreet (D&B) by Requesting a DUNS number with the D&B web form:

http://fedgov.dnb.com/webform.

A Tax Identification Number (TIN) and Taxpayer Name used in Federal tax matters. The TIN is either a Social Security Number or an Employer Identification Number assigned by the Internal Revenue Service. You can request and Request an EIN from the IRS @

http://www.irs.gov/

Get Sponsored

The US Government or a prime contractor can sponsor a registered defense contractor through the security clearance process. This sponsorship occurs when an uncleared contractor wins a classified contract or is otherwise provided a contract vehicle to perform on a classified contract. Prior to performing on the classified contract they must have their FCL and employee PCLs in place and sponsorship is the first step.

Sponsorship supports a valid need to access classified information. I have received many questions about whether or not a company or employee can simply obtain a security clearance for business development purposes, to be "ready" for work, or to be more competitive. The security clearance process begins with a need supported by a legitimate U.S. Government requirement and the classified contract will be offered to meet that need.

During the sponsorship process, the contractor applying for sponsorship and the sponsor complete and submit the following forms to their CSO.

Department of Defense Security Agreement (DD Form 441)

This security agreement is signed between the US Government and defense contractor. It is legally binding and designates responsibilities of each party to follow procedures established by NISPOM. The agreement states that the Government will provide security clearances, properly mark classified information and provide what the cleared contractor needs to perform on the classified contracts. The applying contractor agrees to protect classified information as required by the government.

Certificate Pertaining to Foreign Interests (SF 328)

Cleared contractors are evaluated for the level (if any) of Foreign

Ownership Control or Influence (FOCI) based on the completed SF 328. They should not fall under the influence, control or ownership of a foreign entity to the extent that it causes classified information to be in jeopardy of unauthorized disclosure. Cleared contractors that fall under FOCI can still compete for and perform on classified work; however, there are measures to be taken to ensure that only U.S. persons control the scope of classified work. The CSO and the GCA will be involved in the process.

Business Organization Credentials

One of the responsibilities the contractor applying for a Facility Security Clearance has is to demonstrate that the organization has the history and or the capability to be entrusted with sensitive and classified information. In other words, they must be in good standing. This includes, legal, ethical, and business standings. Every aspect of the business is subject to review and the listed information should be readily available as requested.

Working on classified contracts involves the ability to make good decisions and able to develop security programs to protect classified and sensitive information. The CSO will perform a vulnerability assessment during the sponsorship process and regularly at intervals once the FCL is granted. The good standing reputation must be firmly established and without doubt that it will continue the life of the security clearance.

The company should prove that they are structured and a legal entity under the laws of the United States, the District of Columbia or Puerto Rico and have a physical location in the United States or territories. Such proof includes Articles of Incorporation, Stock Records, Minutes of Board Meetings, and Corporate by-laws. These artifacts will allow the sponsor, GSA, and CSO to better evaluate the sponsored entity to determine ability to protect classified information. Legal and structured business entities include one or more of the following business structures:

Sole Proprietorship

A Sole Proprietorship is a business owned by one individual. The owner is in control of all equipment, supplies and assets of the business. As a result, they receive all the money earned. They control all decisions and are ultimately the single entity committing the business to decisions. The upside is that the owner receives all the benefits and earnings and has full control.

The owner is ultimately responsible for every decision made. They are also liable for any obligations that may extend beyond the business. The business depends 100 percent on the owner's involvement and the owner depends 100 percent on the business' to succeed. This structure may be the easiest as far as managing classified information and security clearances as only one person may be employed.

Partnership

Partnerships exist when two or more people, entities or businesses form a business entity. The partnership formed is independent of the individuals engaged in the partnership. The organizations that form a partnership are a new entity. Depending on the type of partnership, the new entity receives the rewards, benefits and liability of business decisions.

Partners make the day to day decisions of the enterprise and should be prepared to make security clearance decisions. This works well when partners are of the same mind and have the same goals. It can be a frustrating experience when these goals are not clear, personalities conflict and creativity is stifled. Partners should outline the duties ahead of time to determine who is responsible for not only creativity, marketing, sales and other business decisions, but for security and security clearance issues as well.

Corporation

A corporation is a business owned by one or more legal entities. The entities can be other corporations, businesses, individuals, or partnerships. The corporate entities are separate from the individuals who make up that corporation. Corporations offer the best legal protection as the corporation and not the members are accountable. All success and failure affects the corporation and not the individual. The owners and shareholders of corporations are those who own stocks. Each shareholder owns a percentage of the company depending on amount of stocks owned.

Decision making begins with the election of a board of directors. This board of directors determines the direction and company strategy. They hire and appoint company officers to take care of the day to day work. Presidents, Chief Operation Officers, Chief Executive Officers, Vice-Presidents and etc. are hired by the board of directors.

The Key Management Personnel are identified for security clearance decisions and must be designated for review by the CSO. This list may be lengthy for the Corporation as they have many employees and shareholders who may make decisions that impact the management of classified material and security clearances.

Limited Liability Company (LLC)

An LLC structure offers similar benefits and protection as a corporation and the individual in an LLC is protected much better than with a sole proprietorship. The company is controlled either by one or more owners. These owners can be individuals, corporations or other LLCs. The owners can control the company or the owners can appoint managers to control company operations.

An LLC can have a single owner and have all the business making decisions that come from a sole proprietorship as well as protection enjoyed by corporations. However, the LLC has a limited life cycle.

If you form an LLC with others, any of the owners or designated managers can obligate the company.

List of Key Management Personnel (KMP)

These are management or senior leaders who influence decisions regarding classified contracts. KMPs can be members of the board of directors, vice-presidents, directors or other upper level managers. Also, neither the company nor key managers can be barred from participating in US Government contracts. A review of Federal Acquisition Regulations (FAR) demonstrates the ethics and legal requirements of companies who wish to participate in these contracts.

The Investigation Process

Once a company is sponsored for classified work and meets the requirements as identified above, the CSO can begin the process of investigating the business for the FCL award. In the event of a parent-subsidiary relationship within a corporation, both entities are processed for an FCL separately. Usually, the parent company is granted an FCL at the same or higher level as that of the subsidiary. The CSO should determine whether or not the parent will be cleared or excluded based on mission requirements and the contract. If both need clearances, they will be processed separately and as a result, have different CAGE codes.

The company being sponsored will fall under the National Industrial Security Program (NISP) and National Industrial Security Program Operating Manual (NISPOM) is the guide for DoD cleared contractors. The sooner the company obtains their copy of the NISPOM, the quicker they will begin to understand their expected role in protecting the nation's secrets. The NISPOM can downloaded from the DCSA website at http://www.dcsa.mil. A print version is available @ http//www.redbikepublishing.com.

A critical piece of the sponsorship program revolves around the

CSO having a good understanding of the subject company and their mission. To do this, the will review organizational structure and governance documentation to determine which leadership positions can commit the company and make decisions.

The senior company officer, FSO and other KMPs, as deemed necessary by the CSO, will be processed for a security clearance. This requirement can include board members and committee personnel. Proof of citizenship and other documentation is needed to determine eligibility for a clearance. The other officers and board members may be excluded from the security clearance process if they will not have influence over cleared contractor decisions.

Required forms for facility security clearances

Aside from corporate entity documentation, the CSO will collect and process additional forms during the FCL process. These forms include, but are not limited to the Department of Defense Security Agreement (DD Form 441) and the Certificate Pertaining to Foreign Interests (Standard Form 328). The CSO will advise the contractor on how to fill out the forms and answer any questions the contractor may have.

Department of Defense Security Agreement, DD Form 441

The DD Form 441 is a security agreement between the contractor and the government. It lists the responsibilities of both the cleared contractor and the government. For example, the contractor agrees to implement and enforce the security controls necessary to prevent unauthorized disclosure of classified material in accordance with the NISPOM. The contractor also agrees to verify that the subcontractor, customer, individual and any other person has the proper need to know and possesses the security clearance necessary prior to accessing classified information.

The U.S. Government agrees to notify the contractor of the security classification level assigned to classified information. The agreement states that the government will not over classify material and that they will notify the cleared contractor of any changes in the classification level. The Government will also instruct the contractor on the proper handling, storage and disposition of classified material. The Government also agrees to provide security clearances to eligible contractor employees. Classification and classified contract information is found in the contract related Security Classification Guide (SCG) and DD Form 254, both of which are discussed in detail in the book *DoD Security Clearances and Contracts Guidebook*.

The Government will also assess the contractor's ability to protect classified material. For the DoD, this is done through an audit or review performed by the CSO. The CSO will make an initial determination of a contractor's ability to protect classified information. They will also assess and review at reasonable intervals the security process; procedures and methods the cleared facilities use and determine whether or not they are in compliance with the NISPOM. Typically, they use a checklist and the FSO's security plan. These events are scheduled every 12 months for cleared facilities possessing classified information and 18 months for non-possessing facilities. If the cleared contractor is found not in compliance with NISPOM, the GCA or prime contractor will be notified in a written report.

Appendage to Department of Defense Security Agreement, DD

Form 441-1

The DD Form 441-1 is an additional document for use with multiple facility and parent subsidiary companies. The DD Form 441-1 is an additional form providing the government information about the cleared branches or divisions of an organization. These divisions and branches are also included on the DD Form 441 and the SF 328 and information about the companies should be completed as accurately as possible.

Certificate Pertaining to Foreign Interests, Standard Form (SF) 328

The SF 328 is used by the contractor and the CSO to determine whether or not and to what extent the cleared contractor falls under Foreign Ownership Control and Influence (FOCI). The primary concern is always protecting classified information from unauthorized disclosure. As with determining the amount of control a company officer or board member has over classified contracts, the same holds true of foreign entities with which a company may become involved.

In today's global economy it is not unusual for a cleared company to be involved with international business or even be owned by a Non-U.S. entity. If classified contracts are under the control of a foreign entity, the classified information could be in jeopardy of unauthorized disclosure. If a contractor falls under FOCI, the CSO will work with the GCA to evaluate the contractor's ability to mitigate the extent of foreign influence concerning classified information and approve, deny or revoke the FCL.

The SF 328 only has to be completed once unless circumstances change with the contractor. The following is only to be used as a guide and to help the defense contractor understand the types of questions they will need to answer. All coordination should be made with DSS or similar cognizant security agency. An SF 328 can be found online @

https://www.dcsa.mil/mc/ctp/foci/

Maintaining the facility security clearance

A facility clearance follows the life cycle of the classified contract. Close coordination and consultation with the CSO can help with the speedy processing of the FCL. If DSS determines the company is eligible for access to classified information, they will award the appropriate security level. At that point the company can begin the process of personnel security clearance requests and putting procedures in place required to perform on classified work.

The FCL is a determination that a legal entity is trustworthy and able to safeguard classified information. This FCL relates to an organization and not a physical location or building. For example, a cleared contractor organization can move locations and keep the FCL and the clearance remains in place until either party terminates it. If for some reason the contractor no longer requires access, can no longer protect classified information, and is no longer eligible for access to classified material or either party terminates the FCL, the contractor must return or destroy any classified material and provide proof to the GCA.

Summary

A defense contractor is required to have an FCL to perform work on a classified contract. The FCL is not a requirement to bid on classified contracts, but the process of the FCL is initiated upon award of the contract. A company cannot process their own clearance for the sake of looking competitively attractive, but is a result of sponsorship by the Government or a prime contractor. The FCL is strictly contract based and demonstrates an enterprise' trustworthiness to work on classified contracts.

PERSONNEL SECURITY CLEARANCES

S everal years ago this author was a guest on a radio broadcast. I was invited to discuss the security clearance process and how Cleared Defense Contractors (CDC) performed on classified contracts; or so I thought. I was prepared to provide a discussion of guidance as provided by the National Industrial Security Program Operating Manual (NISPOM). The NISPOM guides the CDCs in developing and executing their security programs to protect classified information.

The discussion never got that far. Instead, the hosts lamented of how rogue CDCs were handling classified information. They could not accept the fact that anyone else other than government entities could be allowed access. What they could not fathom is that there is a set of checks and balances that applies in the security clearance process and how cleared employees of CDCs handle classified information. It is our hope to disabuse the reader of having the same opinions.

The Personnel Security Clearance Process

For starters the security clearance process is effective and begins with the Facility Clearance (FCL) and then to the cleared employee. All classified information is provided to CDCs as a result of a contract. The cleared employees are granted access based on the contract, security clearance level, and need to know.

According to Executive Order 12968—Access to Classified Information, employees should not be granted access to classified information unless they possess a security clearance, have a need to know the classified information involved, received an initial security briefing and have signed a nondisclosure agreement.

As a reminder, all cleared contractors must appoint a Facility Security Officer (FSO). It could be the business owner in a small organization or an employee with an additional duty. The primary qualifications of an FSO are to be a US Citizen and have a PCL at the same level as the FCL. It is possible for an FSO to be the sole employee in the company.

Once a defense contractor is granted a FCL, their designated FSO implements a security program to protect classified in information. Part of that responsibility is to initiate security clearance investigations for employees who require a security clearance.

The contractor and DCSA have joint responsibilities with the PCL process as they do with the FCL process. When the FCL investigation is initiated, the employees should complete a Questionnaire for National Security Positions, also known as Standard Form (SF 86). Part of the process includes ensuring that the applicants are US

Citizens. They should submit the application to the FSO who then submits applications. An investigation is conducted and the central adjudication facility (CAF) makes a security clearance determination.

Over the years I've been asked the same question: "Can you help me get a security clearance? My answer is both yes and no. If the individual either owns a business and is competing for a classified contract or has a contractual need for a Facility Clearance, then they are eligible to pursue a security clearance. Likewise, if they work for a cleared defense contractor and require a security clearance to perform on classified work, then the answer is yes as well.

With that established, I can advise and assist with the security clearance process. For a PCL, the applicant begins with the Questionnaire for National Security Positions or also known as the SF 86. The SF 86 is primarily the part of the process that the applicant can affect the speed of the security clearance process. A properly filled out application form is the key. Incomplete or inaccurate information is the number one cause of clearance delays. Names, addresses, telephone numbers, and dates of birth for relatives should be gathered as background research. Fortunately the SF 86 form is online and requires only filling out once and updating when reinvestigations are required. When a clearance is up for renewal, the applicant can log in their SF 86 and make updates.

Not everyone investigated is guaranteed a security clearance. In some instances a clearance can be denied, revoked or suspended. The employee's background is investigated thoroughly for the initial clearance and again every five to fifteen years while maintaining a clearance and depending on the required security clearance level. In the event that a security clearance is denied, suspended or revoked, the CSO will also notify the FSO. The FSO will then deny access to classified material to that employee.

The personnel security clearance investigation

Prior to granting a security clearance, a thorough security clearance background investigation is conducted. Two primary types of investigation included the Single Scope Background Investigation (SSBI) and the National Agency Check with Local Agency Check and Credit Check (NACLC).

The SSBI

The SSBI is the most detailed investigation and is used to process TOP SECRET (TS), and Sensitive Compartmented Information (SCI) clearances. The FSO initiates the security clearance request and notifies the employee to begin the application by filling completing Electronic Questionnaires for Investigations Processing (e-QIP) Standard Form 86 (SF 86) to verify employment. The federal investigator verifies the information by interviewing references, employers or others who have known the subject socially or professionally. The investigator may use names identified on the SF 86 and as discovered during the course of the investigation. To facilitate an efficient investigation, applicants should complete the SF 86 accurately and completely.

The SSBI will also cover periods of employment and education institutions attended. The applicant should be accurate about the attendance and degrees, certificates or diplomas credited and list contacts or references as completely as possible. Other areas subject to investigation include places of residence, criminal records and involvement with law enforcement and financial records. The investigators may contact those with social and professional knowledge of the applicant, and divorced spouses.

The SSBI is reserved for employees (military, civilian and contractor) requiring a TOP SECRET security clearance and access to sensitive compartmented information (SCI).

Keep in mind that the SCI is not an investigation but an access determination based on an explicit need to access intelligence information, the SSBI investigation and the final adjudication. Once access is granted the applicant will be indoctrinated or "read on". So, SCI is not an investigation it's the access granted after the investigation and is usually referred to as TOP SECRET/SCI.

Since the national security stakes are high, there are more active inquiries occurring than with other investigations for security clearances at the SECRET level or below. The level of scrutiny involved in an SSBI makes it one of the most time consuming and detailed investigations.

The scope of the SSBI investigation goes back 10 years for general information concerning finances, education and professional activities. The investigators will check 7 years back for more personal information such as relationships and character references. Some of the investigative techniques involve running a check to verify:

- The date & place of birth
- National Agency Check into the Department of Defense agencies, FBI, and other databases to see if any derogatory information exists.
- Spouse or cohabitant check to determine allegiance, associations and other factors that a close relationship might bring.
- Credit checks provide more information about the applicant. This query into the major credit trackers can verify residences, identity, financial situations, relationships, patterns and much more.
- Local law enforcement check to identify any arrests or activities involving law enforcement.
- Public records verification to determine associations and activities the applicant may be or has been involved in.
- Citizenship verification to ensure applicant is a US citizen and eligible for a security clearance.

Written Inquiries are provided to education and employment institutions and references to verify education level and employment.

Interviews are conducted based on references provided by the applicant. These interviews include neighbors, former spouses and the actual applicant.

The NACLC

The NACLC is required for SECRET and CONFIDENTIAL levels of security clearances. Investigations are conducted to determine suitability for a clearance, fingerprint classification and a background check using a search of the Federal Bureau of Investigation's (FBI) database. Investigators also conduct a credit check based on residence, employment and education locations. The investigation will also cover law enforcement issues at all locations listed on the SF 86. Once assigned a case, investigators will use the submitted request to research factors about the employee's life to help determine suitability. The suitability is assessed by a trained adjudicator based on an approved background investigation.

The granted security clearance is honored across agencies and no additional investigations should be conducted to access classified information at the same level or lower of the PCL. If an employee has a security clearance granted by any agency with an investigation meeting the same or higher requirements, access to classified information can usually be granted without further investigation.

The Questionnaire for National Security Positions or Standard Form (SF-86).

The SF 86 is a form used to investigate people for security clearances. Completing the form is voluntary, but it is powerful in that it is both necessary to complete for the execution of the security clearance investigation and there can be repercussions if false information is purposefully given. Additionally, it becomes a permanent record.

Failure to provide accurate or complete information or providing false or misleading data could result in denial or delay of a security clearance and or loss of job. Willingly providing false or misleading information could also result in fines or jail time.

The SF 86 has many questions and most require yes or no answers. For some "yes" answers, you should be prepared to list details. This section gives only a recommendation of details you should be prepared to provide based on the SF 86 and is no way meant to represent the actual form. However, it is here to help prepare you to gather the documentation, and points of contact required for the form. Use this as you search letters, address books, files, websites and other sources necessary to complete the SF 86. The actual form can be found @

http://www.opm.gov/forms/pdf_fill/sf86.pdf

This security clearance journey begins with the applicant completing the SF-86 and concludes with the granting of a personnel security clearances (PCL) following a lengthy investigation and adjudication process. The SF-86 is a lengthy form that requires the population of some very personal information to include family members, places lived, academic institutes attended, arrests, drug and alcohol incidents, debt, and more. The investigators refer to the information provided by the applicant to gather, research, follow up, document, and provide to the adjudicators for a security clearance decision.

You should fill out all information completely and accurately. Withholding, misrepresenting, or falsifying information could have detrimental impact and may cost a security clearance or sensitive position denial, future employment and federal employment opportunities and possibly even result in prosecution. Keep in mind that the information put on the initial SF-86 may be compared with SF-86 information provided as a result of future or continuing security clearance investigations.

Facility Security Officers Can Help

The form is completed online and once complete, the applicant should review the form with the Facility Security Officer (FSO). The FSO is the first person to review all the sensitive information with the applicant. The FSO ensures the form is complete, accurate, and all waivers and signatures are applied. FSOs are not decisions makers in the security clearance process and therefore not authorized to pass judgement, make adjudicative calls, or decisions about the clearance request – they are simply reviewing for completeness.

Government Receives and Compiles

Employees of agencies within the security clearance process will then have access to the SF-86 and are required to handle the information in accordance with their responsibilities and according to the Privacy Act. These employees will access the SF-86 while conducting background investigations, reinvestigations, and continuous evaluations of persons under consideration for, or retention of, national security positions. These also include non-investigating employees conducting administration functions. These include contractor and government personnel security clearance employees, investigators, adjudicators and others who have authorization to conduct legitimate business.

SF-86 Becomes Record

Additionally the investigation conducted using information on the SF-86 can be used in studies and analyses to evaluate an agency's effectiveness in applying investigative and adjudicative methodologies. Think about process improvement or reports to congress on government effectiveness.

According to the form itself: "The collection, maintenance, and disclosure of background investigative information are governed by the Privacy Act…. The information you provide on this form, and information collected during an investigation, may be disclosed without your consent by an agency maintaining the information in a system of records as permitted by the Privacy Act..."

The following are those who might view the SF-86 in its entirety:
- Department of Justice in performing their duties
- Courts if litigation is involved for civil or criminal violations
- Employees performing security clearance investigations

The following are those who might view information that is on the SF-86, but will not be able to associate the information with an individual:
- Federal, state, local, foreign, tribal or other public authority as appropriate
- Contractors, grantees, experts, consultants or volunteers as they cooperate in the investigation
- News media or general public for factual information, but not PII
- Congress, national archives, foreign governments, office of management and budget

Providing information is voluntary, but failure to complete the form will result in disqualification of the process. Since the form is the trigger, the starting gun is never fired and the runners never get off the starting line. If an SF-86 is not completed, the process is never started. Also, if an applicant does not provide all of the requested information it could negatively affect their eligibility for a national security position or access to classified information.

Again this SF-86 completion should take a few hours which is achievable if you are prepared to answer the questions. However, most who see the form for the first time are not able to immediately access the information they need. If unprepared, the applicant could spend valuable time gathering relevant information. If you have moved frequently, have a large family, travel internationally, change jobs frequently, have multiple financial transactions, this could take some digging to find all the relevant information.

For example, say a person has moved 8 times in a 10 year period. Not only do they list their residences, but also must include their neighbor's name and contact information. If that same person has had multiple employers, they would need to list employment addresses as well as supervisor names and contact information.

Some things you can do to speed up your security clearance process includes gathering all the information listed below as well as check and fix any legal, civil or credit issue. It still takes time to get the information and resolve issues. However, if your plans include getting a security clearance, do the work now so that when you apply, you'll have the information up front. Go ahead and download a fillable SF-86 and get started. Save it on your computer for the day you need it.

Additionally, take care of any open credit, civil, or legal issues. For example, if you have a security freeze on your consumer or credit report file, you should request that the consumer reporting agencies lift the freeze in these instances to avoid security clearance investigation stalls.

Other people may be included in the investigation

The form asks for information about yourself, neighbors, employers, family members and current and former spouses. Investigative checks may be conducted on relatives, former and current spouses, and other references you may have annotated.

Lots of SF-86 Questions and Very Little Intuitive Knowledge

Questions on the SF-86 have a purpose. The purpose may be a mystery to members of the general public. Many questions appear to be vague and without explanation. You will probably have a lot of questions about what questions are asked or how to answer the questions. Maybe the following statement will be of comfort and aid in understanding the intent:

The purpose of the investigation is to determine suitability; not disqualify people.

For example, there are a ton of questions about foreign contact. The questions leave room for a ton of answers. You will have to read the interpretation of what a foreign contact is as well as how many you should list. The quantity of contacts are not an issue. At issue is whether you are honest about your contacts and whether or not your decisions can be coerced by foreign influence.

The purpose is not to exclude applicants who actually have foreign contacts, so go ahead and list them. It's better to caution on the side of too much information. It's easier to mitigate security clearance issue than it is to mitigate deception or falsifying records (SF-86).

During the investigation, investigators may conduct interview with you. During the interview you can ask question, explain your answers to any question, or make clarification of your listed information. The interview can provide an opportunity to update, clarify, and explain information on your form more completely, which often assists in completing your investigation.

Clarification can also be made after the final determination on your eligibility for the security clearance. If your security clearance is denied, you will be provided the opportunity to explain, refute, or clarify any information before a final decision is made, if an unfavorable decision is considered.

Preparing to Complete the SF-86

Be prepared to do a lot of research on where you have travelled, lived, studied, worked. Be sure to provide specific addresses and phone numbers of not only the locations, but neighbors, relatives, and people who can validate the information provided. For some, this could prove to be a lot of research that you can begin to gather now. Thankfully the internet and other resources are available for the research. If you have the time and available internet resources, you should be able to get most if not all of the required information.

White pages, maps, address books, and other information are available on popular internet web browsers. Sometimes all you need to remember is a name and a general location. Also, social networks provide a rich place to search for hard to remember information.

The first sections of the SF-86 is all about your identity and citizenship. Requested information includes name, other names used, methods of identification such as social security number or passport. After identification, the applicant will have to complete information on citizenship. This includes whether or not the applicant is a U.S. citizen, how citizenship was established, dual citizenship and a section if the applicant is not a U.S. citizen. A driver's license, social security number, passport, citizenship documents and perhaps or other means of identification can be used to validate the application.

Next, list residences over the past 10 years. Gather information of where you have lived and be sure to use actual physical addresses such as a house or apartment number. Provide the current address and phone number of a neighbor who knew you at that address.

Next, provide information on where you attended school, if any, during the last 10 year period. If so, put the name of school, month and year attended and whether or not you received a degree or diploma. One recommended resource is the website:

http://ope.ed.gov/accreditation/search.aspx

This provides relevant information on education institutes. Provide the current address and phone number of someone who knew you at the school.

Next, provide employment information. Collect information on where you worked during the last 10 years. This includes all part time and full time employment and military service. List the name of the employer and dates worked. Also, provide the current address and phone number of someone who can verify your employment. There is an additional section for military service. You will need to refer to your military service records such as DD Form 214 if this section applies.

Provide names and contact information for three people who know you well. These cannot be relatives, spouses, former spouses nor anyone who you may have listed in other sections of the SF-86. They can be neighbors, friends, colleagues and etc who can speak of your activities and actions during the previous seven years.

The marriage and family relationship sections require potentially a lot of information on potential many people. For marriages, unions, partnerships and etc, you should be prepared to provide names, contact information, citizenship, and, status of the relationship. If you have been or currently are married or have lived with someone as married, provide name, address, social security number and citizenship of current spouse, former spouses or anyone you may have lived with as a spouse. This should include any civil unions or anything that resembles cohabitation and any divorces, separations or a civil dissolution of the relationship. If not U.S. persons, you will have to list nationality, frequency and type of contact.

You will also need information on members of immediate family whether or not they are living or deceased. Include parents, step-parents, guardians, foster parents, siblings, step-siblings, half-siblings, children, step-children, fathers and mothers in-law. You should have addresses and phone numbers for all living relatives, dates and places of birth, citizenship documentation. If not U.S. persons, you will have to list nationality, frequency and type of contact.

The remaining sections ask questions reflecting the 13 Adjudicative Criteria discussed earlier. If applicable, list information about foreign contacts, drugs and alcohol involvement, counseling, information technology usage, law enforcement issues, debt, and the rest. It may be intimidating and lengthy, but again, be complete and thorough. Though there are certain conditions where an applicant may be categorically disqualified for a clearance, most issues can be "adjudicated". In other words, the whole person concept is applied before a determination is made. Even though there may be red flags at some points in an applicants experience, the events could be overlooked based on how long ago the events occurred, current behavior, counseling, and other positive change.

Foreign Involvement-Continuing, provide information for any foreign contacts you may have had during the last 7 years. List names, citizenship, addresses, phone numbers, nature of relationship, type of contact and frequency of contact.

The next section is about your own foreign activities to include relationships, business and financial transactions, support of others, political involvement and foreign travel and etc. Be prepared to provide addresses, phone numbers, account and property information of financial and business activity. For foreign country visits, list locations, dates and purposes of the visits.

Psychological and Emotional Health-If you have been treated or diagnosed by a professional or other circumstances you will need to complete this section. The SF 86 also requires dates, treatment location and the provider of any mental health counseling.

Police Record-List the date, court location, offense and action taken for any police record activity during last 7 years. This includes charges or records that were expunged, stricken from the record or dismissed.

Illegal Drug Use and Drug Activity-Provide information on illegal drug use by date, type of drug and nature of drug use. This should cover the last 7 years. Information you provide includes reason for drug use and whether or not you intend to use drugs again.

Alcohol Incidents-Include information of alcohol use that has affected your ability to perform on the job, affected relationships, has resulted in mandatory or voluntary counseling. List detailed information on the incidents and if received counseling, provided name of counselor, dates and location.

Background Investigations-If the US or a foreign government has investigated your background, be prepared to provide the date, agency and government investigating and the type of security clearance.

Financial Information-Disclose any financial obligations that you have assumed during the last 7 years. This includes account numbers, and organization that any debt is or was owed. Be prepared to provide detailed information on situations where you did not meet loan agreements or financial obligations.

Use of Information Technology System Use-Provide information where during the last 7 years you have illegally or without authorization entered into an information technology system, modified, destroyed, manipulated or denied someone access, or otherwise misused information technology systems. List the date, nature, location and action taken concerning each offense.

Non-Criminal Court Activity-If you have been involved in any non criminal court activity the last 7 years list the date, nature and result of action, involved parties and court location.

Associations Record-Complete this section for whether or not you have knowingly or unknowingly contributed or supported those involved in terrorism, overthrow of the U.S. Government or suppressed civil rights of U.S. citizens.

Finally, you will sign the SF-86 and give approval for investigators to review medical and other records during the course of the investigation.

Periodic Reinvestigations

The granted security clearance is part of a continuing evaluation process. Once a security clearance is granted the cleared employee will be periodically reevaluated and re investigated if the clearance is to remain in effect. When cleared employees require access to classified material beyond the scope of the initial investigation, the security office will submit a request for a Periodic Reinvestigation (PR). The adjudicator makes decisions concerning whether or not the subject's allegiance is still to the United States, they can still be trusted to protect classified information and they will still be able to carry out their duties at all times.

The PR for the TOP SECRET clearance is the same level of investigation as was initially conducted. The SSBI-PR is conducted every 5 years as needed. For SECRET, the NACLC is conducted every 10 years and for CONFIDENTIAL the NACLC is conducted every 15 years. Part of the security education process emphasizes the importance of continuous evaluation of the cleared employee. This is a requirement for cleared employees to report any information on themselves and other cleared employees that may demonstrate an inability to protect classified information.

Actions to Take

Applicants can speed up the investigation and adjudication process by providing complete and accurate information on their SF 86. Any unexplained anomalies, mistakes or omissions could cause a delay or denial of the security clearances.

If a security clearance is in your future, you could begin collecting data now and practice completing the unofficial SF-86 found at _http://www.opm.gov/forms/pdf_fill/sf86.pdf_ before you actually need it. Then you can have all the information at hand when it is time to complete the official paperwork. Information about schools, references, friends, banks, former employers, foreign contacts, relations, and etc may not be readily available and collecting that data could take a lot of time. If a security clearance job is the goal, the applicant should begin gathering the information as soon as possible. Names, addresses, phone numbers should be accurate and through. Use transcripts, letters, records and the internet to collect the data.

The Adjudicative Process

Whether considering an initial investigation or a PR, the adjudicative process requires an authority to consider all evidence and make a decision of whether or not a person is suitable to have a security clearance. The adjudicator weighs decisions based on information the subject provided in the SF 86 as well as the results of the investigation. The adjudicator will use the information to determine whether or not the person is stable, reliable or subject to coercion based on the whole person concept. The whole person concept allows an assessment of many factors that may help mitigate negative findings. These include:

The nature, extent, and seriousness of the conduct

There are varying degrees of impact and circumstances of individual conduct. Looking at each incident case by case will provide better details useful in determining whether or not a person is given security clearance.

The circumstances surrounding the conduct

There are situations that may cause someone to take adverse action. People under stress, duress or threat react in different ways.

The frequency and of the conduct and when it occurred

Conduct may be habitual or a onetime incident. Adjudicators can use the information discovered to make a better determination. For example, a subject has a record of drug counseling from twenty years earlier. The incident occurred in the past and was a onetime occurrence.

The individual's age and maturity at the time of the conduct

Minors are not held accountable for their actions the same way as adults. For example, a subject had several moving violations during the first year after obtaining a driver's license. Incidents may have resulted from immaturity and not a reflection of who the person is now.

The willingness to participate

People can be coerced into doing things they do not want to do. Some people volunteer freely to commit crimes or engage in risky behavior. Both situations are taken into account during the adjudication process. For example, a subject joins a group hostile to the US Government after an invitation is extended; they volunteered freely. Coercion involves a person forced to engage in adverse behavior to avoid certain consequences.

The presence or absence of rehabilitation and other pertinent behavioral changes

Adjudicators may consider whether or not the subject sought counseling or other psychological help with addiction, grief, anger and other behavior issues that can affect the ability to obtain a security clearance. For example, a subject receives counseling to manage their anger.

The motivation for the conduct

The adjudicator may consider the reasons a person behaved adversely. Justice, revenge, anger, self-defense or duress are examples of different types of motivation that can change behavior. For example, a subject attacks and injures a bystander only after friend plies them with alcohol.

The potential for pressure, coercion, exploitation, or duress

There are some situations that can make people vulnerable; peer pressure, alcohol or drug tolerance, coercion and exploitation is a few. These are also taken into consideration to determine whether or not a security clearance and an applicants' situation would create vulnerability. In an earlier example, a subject married to a foreign national from an oppressive country may be coerced to help an adversary obtain privileged information.

The likelihood of continuation or recurrence

Information on a subject is used to determine whether or not the behavior will happen again. For example, a person had been in counseling for an alcohol related event. Both the counseling and the alcohol related event occurred 15 years prior. Since then there have been no further indicators of alcohol abuse. The adjudicator may determine that the likelihood of recurrence is low. Each case will be judged on its own merits, and any doubt concerning personnel being considered for access to classified information will be resolved in favor of national security.

What happens when the security clearance is granted

Once the adjudication provides favorable results, DSS notifies the FSO through JPAS. However, the FSO should ensure the employee receives an initial security briefing, signs a SF 312 Classified Information Non-Disclosure Agreement and has a need to know relating to a contract or job description. The training of newly cleared employees begins with a briefing of their responsibilities to protect classified information and as outlined on the Classified Information Nondisclosure Agreement or SF 312.

The SF 312 is an agreement between the cleared employee and the U.S. government outlining both parties' responsibilities to protect our nation's secrets. The FSO does not grant a newly cleared employee access to classified information or program until the employee is trained and signs the SF 312. Once the SF 312 is signed by both the employee and witness, the FSO will forward it through JPAS to DSS.

During the security clearance investigation process, the U.S. Government investigates the background of a candidate to determine the applicant's suitability to protect classified information. Depending on the security clearance level, the investigation and adjudication process can be lengthy. While the investigation continues to determine a final clearance, the U.S. Government may grant a temporary and limited interim clearance at the Confidential, Secret, or Top Secret levels.

Interim Security Clearances

An interim clearance is a temporary and limited granting of access to classified information. This is a privilege that allows an applicant to perform on classified work in a temporary capacity until their background investigation is completed. It is routinely granted during a security clearance investigation and ends immediately upon the conclusion of the investigation – with either a clearance grant or denial.

The interim clearance does not have a time constraint, but is tied to the investigation. If the investigation does not determine any adverse information, the interim clearance may be granted. While the formal investigation can take many months, interim clearances have been granted within days of the original security clearance investigation request.

An interim clearance will remain in effect until the final clearance is determined, or adverse information is discovered. For example, if an applicant has an interim clearance granted at the Secret level, their status will continue to be interim until granted the final clearance. Once the final clearance at the Secret level is granted, the interim is no longer necessary. If the final determination is a clearance denial, the interim clearance will also cease.

Applicants who are granted interim security clearances at the Confidential and Secret levels can access Confidential and Secret information.

Likewise, those provided interim Top Secret security clearances will be authorized access to Top Secret information.

Those with Interim Secret and Confidential clearances are not eligible to access Restricted Data, NATO Information, and COMSEC information.

Those with interim Top Secret are only eligible to access Restricted Data, NATO Information, and COMSEC information at the Secret and Confidential levels.

Technically, if an employee changes employment in the middle of an investigation, the investigation can continue as long as the need to perform on a classified contract exists. If an interim clearance is granted, it will follow the employee to the next cleared contractor facility (if there is still a need).

If you consult a few Facility Security Officers (FSOs) about this, you're likely to get theoretical answers – since not too many people change jobs within a few months of hire. For an interim to be granted in a matter of hours and a final to be granted in months, it would be pretty rare for an employee to seek a new position during the interim clearance period.

What you can do when a security clearance is denied

Interim security clearances are granted almost immediately if there is no immediate derogatory information. A candidate who has no issues can be granted an interim clearance and can begin work almost immediately as long as the interim clearance is at the level of classified information being worked. However, if an interim clearance is denied, the applicant will have to wait until the full investigation is complete and a clearance approved before performing on a classified contract. A denied interim clearance does not equate to a denied security clearance.

If after the course of investigation, the adjudicator determines that a clearance cannot be granted, they will notify the applicant. The applicant will intern have a recourse.

The appeal process begins with the Defense Office of Hearings and Appeals (DOHA). The denied individual can request to see the DOHA administrative judge to provide supporting documentation, or additional information as well as question information found during the investigation. At that point the judge makes a decision.

If the denial stands, the denied individual can go to the Appeal Board. Once the Appeal Board weighs in, the decision is final. If the decision supports the denial, the applicant cannot reapply for a year. If the employee's job position still requires a clearance, the employee should present supporting information during the reapplication process.

What to while waiting for the investigation and adjudication

While waiting on a security clearance, the applicant cannot perform on classified information. The best case, the employer will determine that the employee is worth the wait and allow them to perform in an unclassified capacity until the clearance is granted. The individual should show value to the organization and perform well, provide supporting documents and continue to conduct themselves in a trustworthy manner.

Drug Tests

Drug Involvement is one of the 13 adjudicative criteria which could lead to the denial or revocation of a security clearance. Even so, marijuana and opioids continue to be a concern for many applicants.

Drug involvement can raise questions about loyalty, reliability, and ability to protect classified information for initial security clearance assessments, it is a strong possibility that you can be tested for drug at some point in the security clearance process.

For initial security clearances, a drug test may be required after the SF-86 is completed. This would not be a part of the standard security clearance process, but a suitability requirement triggered by the agency granting eligibility.

Implications of a "Failed" Drug Test

The results of a positive or "failed" drug test are devastating. A "failed" drug test will provide enough information to revoke a security clearance. While it may be possible to fight the results – the chances are slim. The bottom line is that cleared employees should begin and remain drug free.

Employee suitability vs security clearance suitability

Government agencies and their cleared defense contractors require drug testing or screening prior to hiring new employees to address the issues of the employee's suitability. Regardless of the security clearance needs, the new employee is often required to test as part of the hiring process. For example, a cleared employee changing jobs most likely will take a drug test while changing employers, as would the non-cleared employees. However, the same cleared employee may not be required to take a drug test while remaining at their current job. Cleared employees may experience random drug testing as part of an internal requirement as would non-cleared employees, but there are no consistent requirements for ongoing testing (they're often called random for a reason).

The Continuous Evaluation Process

Cleared personnel should also continue their demonstration of suitability after the security clearance is determined. Cleared employees are responsible for notifying their security offices anytime they or another cleared employee violate any of the criteria. This is referred to as reporting adverse information. Failure to report adverse information could result in risk to national security and could manifest during the PR. For example, adverse information discovered on a subject during the PR that should have been self-reported, may raise questions of trustworthiness. Self reporting of adverse information demonstrates trustworthiness and helps mitigate the event's impact.

SUMMARY

A PCL is the administrative determination that an employee is eligible from a national security basis for a security clearance. The PCL is based on a contract and the FCL. The FSO provides justification for an employee clearance and submits a clearance request to DSS who then assigns an investigation based on the clearance level. The investigations are thorough and based on 13 criteria to determine eligibility. Once the investigation is complete, the clearance request will go through an adjudication process.

AFTER THE SECURITY CLEARANCE

Remembering the distinction between the Cleared Defense
Contractor (CDC) and the cleared employee, we will proceed
with explaining what happens to each once a clearance is
granted. We are describing this from two points of view; a brand new
CDC or business with a newly granted clearance and a newly cleared
employee of any given CDC

THE CLEARED DEFENSE CONTRACTOR

Once the defense contractor has its first classified contract, they become a Cleared Defense Contractor and can begin to develop a secu-

rity program to protect classified information based on the requirements provided by the Government Contracting Agency or the prime contractor. Whenever the government or prime contractor awards a classified contract to a cleared contractor or cleared subcontractor, they specify the highest level of classified information and the required safeguarding methods. This security guidance is provided in the Contract Security Classification Specification DD Form 254 and is provided to identify the type of classified work the cleared contractor is expected to perform, the classification level of the work to be performed and how the classified information should be protected while under the cleared contractor's control.

The appointed Facility Security Officer (FSO) should develop the security plan in concert with other company business units including contracts, engineers, program managers or other relevant departments to ensure all aspects of business are captured to insert the security plan into company culture. The National Security Program Operating Manual (NISPOM) requires the guides the cleared defense contractor (CDC) to provide input to the DD Form 254 and how it to apply guidance at the CDC facility. The FSO should review the DD Form 254 with affected cleared employees to ensure it is accurate, clear and that everyone performing on the contract understands the security requirements. Additionally, the FSO should ensure they receive the classification guidance I the Security Classification Guide (SCG) from the customer. The SCG is program specific and may spell out detailed information that facilitates the identification and protection of classified information.

The FSO is the point of contact with the Cognizant Security Office (CSO) and should ensure that the CDC abides by requirements in the DD Form 254, SCG and NISPOM. It is the cleared contractor's responsibility to ensure the organization understands and applies the security requirements provided and the CSO will inspect the CDC based on how well they apply NISPOM guidance to the classified contract.

FSO responsibilities include providing a good assessment of any security product and service costs necessary to meet requirements. While the government pays for the security clearance process, provides the classified material, and government funded equipment, the CDC incurs the costs required to protecting the classified information. For example, the defense contractor agrees to abide by the NISPOM and therefore is expected to bring their facilities up to the level necessary to protect the classified information. Therefore, the CDC should consider costs required to implement the NISPOM. These costs include alarms, GSA Approved Security Containers, staff, dedicated facility space, and office equipment required to mail, document, destroy or otherwise handle the disposition of classified material.

THE CLEARED EMPLOYEE

Congratulations to the newly cleared employee. The government has made the decision to grant the security clearance and they are now eligible to work on classified contracts. This privilege comes with a huge responsibility for them to both continue to conduct themselves in line with the 13 Adjudicative Guidelines protecting their continued eligibility as well as protecting the classified information under their charge from unauthorized access. The standards as to which the applicant was adjudicated is what will be used to ensure they remain eligible to maintain the security clearance. Depending on the security clearance level granted, they will undergo a continuous evaluation process as well as several future iterations of re-investigations.

Once an employee receives their security clearance, the owning Facility Security Officer (FSO) will begin to inject them into the enterprise security program designed to protect classified information. This security plan is both over arching in application as well as tailored to the specific contractual requirements provided by the Government Contracting Agency or the prime contractor. This is a flowed down requirement and is applied when the government or prime contractor awards a classified contract to a cleared contractor or cleared subcontractor and the requirements are flowed down to the lowest tiered contractor. As such, they specify the highest level of classified information the cleared employee will have access to and any required or special safeguarding methods. This security guidance is addressed in a document called Contract Security Classification Specification or DD Form 254 and is provided to identify the type of classified work you as a cleared employee are expected to perform, the classification level of the work to be performed and how the classified information should be protected while under their control.

The classified information accessed could come in various forms and media. It could be hardcopy print material, reside on a computer, be in a software or hardware format, reside on a drive or removable platform or be a piece of machinery, vehicle or something else. It is important for careers, job security and national security that everyone understands what is expected while have access to and possessing the classified information in whatever format it exists. If anyone causes the unauthorized release of classified information, they could contribute to various levels of damage to national security. It is critical that everyone makes it their business to you pay attention to training and briefings so that their is a good understand how to execute those duties and continue to enjoy the newfound privilege.

INTERPRETING REQUIREMENTS IN THE DD FORM 254 AND NISPOM

The costs associated with performing on classified contracts will vary by contract and depends on whether or not the CDC is a possessing or non-possessing facility. The possessing facility is one that performs classified work at the CDC location and may require the storage of classified documents or material at the CDC facility. Depending on the contract, this could involve purchasing multiple security containers or acquiring large storage areas for oversized material such as weapons systems or computers. For non-possessing facilities, this does not require the storage of classified information at the CDC. However, the CDC will provided cleared employees to perform classified work at locations other than at the CDC facility.

The FSO can help reduce costs associated with protecting classified information by being involved and preparing as early in the acquisition process as possible. This is where an experience FSO can anticipate expenses, perform risk assessment while implementing NISPOM, and advise on ways to reduce costs while being compliant. The more money saved on overhead expenses, the greater the overall company profit. The earlier into the process the assessment is conducted the better the company performs. Conducting a cost impact study or coordinating with the GCA and CSO later than necessary may place the contractor in the tough position of last minute work and higher associated expenses while building closed areas, ordering more GSA approved containers (safes), and meeting tough governmental compliance with short notice.

One good idea is for the FSO to form a working team to consider the costs. These could be program managers, engineers, security, contract and other managers responsible for developing business with the prime contractor or GCA. This team would consider the contract, security requirements, have decision authority and the ability to commit the company to the developing security plan. The FSO contributes by providing information and guidance on protecting classified information in the process and such planning could translate into significant cost reduction.

Understanding how to advise and assist in the development of the DD Form 254 and SCG brings the CDC into the planning process early and can benefit the government and the CDC by reducing time and resources. It provides the ground work for ensuring the customer security requirements are clear, applicable, and understood. Since the government provides the protection requirements, getting in on the ground level development can only benefit the contractor.

The FSO can use the DD Form 254 requirements as a baseline in assessing the current state of security to determine whether or not the company has enough classified storage space, the right type of storage space, whether or not alarms are needed and other physical security needs to support the contract, and the adequate security or support staff is on hand. Other performance requirements may indicate the need for classified computer processing, upgrading facility and personnel clearances, and increasing storage level and capability.

CDC Training Requirements; FSO Certification

One of the many NISPOM requirements CDCs should follow and document the accomplishment is the implementation of security and refresher training. Training should occur immediately upon contract award so the structure is in place to execute appropriate security compliance. A well trained FSO and cleared employee staff can begin to protect classified information and contracts well before performance starts. Documenting the training during the initial CSO review will also assist with the overall vulnerability rating and demonstrate willingness to protect classified information appropriately.

The DD Form 254 could specify security training and briefings at levels above CONFIDENTIAL, SECRET, and TOP SECRET. This information includes COMSEC, Intelligence, NATO and other categories that could require briefings first to the FSO and then to the cleared employees including engineers, program managers, and senior managers performing on the classified work. Depending on the requirements, the CSO may provide additional briefings to the FSO such as for the mentioned categories. In turn, the FSO will be expected to provide the same briefings to designated cleared employees.

FSOs are expected to provide cleared employees with initial and refresher training. Instead of conducting training just to meet compliance, the training can be performed as an effective relationship building opportunity. This education increases a cleared employee's knowledge of responsibility to protect classified material; detect attempts at espionage and other security violations; and report incidents, violations and status changes affecting personnel and facility clearances.

Training should be contract specific to protect the classified information while meeting the customer's needs. Training topics include familiarization with the SCG, details corresponding to topics in the DD Form 254, and a refresher of the initial security training topics as they could be impacted with the new work.

The CSO provides initial training and special briefings to the FSO. The FSO is then authorized to provide the training to the cleared employees. According to NISPOM, the FSO is also required to participate either online or on site in the FSO Program Management Course within one year of appointment. Either way the CDC chooses to train the FSO, the FSO must be certified and present credentials during the CSO reviews.

The government provides online and in residence courses designed for FSOs of possessing and non-possessing facilities. FSOs should coordinate with their CSO representative to determine the training that's right for their situation. The training is designed to prepare the FSO to implement and direct a NISPOM based security program in their cleared contractor facility including, but not limited to the following topics which are also discussed in detail in the book DoD Security Clearance and Contracts Guidebook:

Protecting classified material – Protect classified material during receipt, accountability, storage, dissemination and destruction.

Required training topics – Establishes an ongoing training program designed to create an environment of security conscious cleared employees. Required training topics are discussed in the next section.

Personnel security clearances – Provides an understanding of the personnel security clearance request procedure, briefing techniques and maintenance of personnel clearances.

Facility clearances – Teaches how FCLs are established and which records and activities are required to maintain the FCL.

Foreign Ownership Control and Influence (FOCI) – Analyzes CDC foreign investments, sales and ownership on a regular basis using the Certificate Pertaining to Foreign Interests (SF 328). FSOs learn to interact with management and provide guidance and direction in preventing a foreign entity from unauthorized access to or controlling work involving classified and export controlled information.

Exports Compliance And International Operations –Instructs on how to prevent unauthorized disclosure of critical technology, classified and export controlled information. Focuses on topics in the International Traffic in Arms Regulation (ITAR)

Restricted Areas – Teaches how designated areas can be established to control temporary access to classified material.

Closed Areas – Teaches how to store and work with classified material in a dedicated space. This involves approved construction and limited accesses controls to prevent unauthorized disclosure during and after work hours.

Contract Security Classification Specification (DD Form 254) – Teaches how to read and apply the DD Form 254. The cleared contractor is allowed access to classified contracts based on the DD Form 254. The FSO would learns how the DD Form 254 is constructed and how to provide input to better meet security requirements.

Security Classification Guides (SCG) – Instructs on reviewing and applying classification to classified products. As the DD Form 254 provides authorization to execute a classified contract, the SCG provides the "how to" instruction.

Security Administration And Records Keeping – Teaches the maintenance of facility and personnel security clearance information as well as all other accountability. The FSO is expected to provide information on personnel clearances, original documentation of their facility clearance and demonstrate classified information accountability during the DSS annual security inspection.

Sub-contracting – Teaches how to flow down classified work requirements to sub-contractors. When approved to subcontract classified work, the prime contractor will provide a DD Form 254 to the subcontractor.

The government issues training certificates which should be filed for presentation during security audits. The FSO training should not end with this course. Career enhancing training is available through various security and management courses. More in depth online and residence training is available in each above mentioned topic. Other agencies may offer more training certification in special access programs, COMSEC, and intelligence protection. Other training is available in colleges, professional organizations, vendor websites, through books like this and within the security community.

CDC Training Requirements; Cleared Employee Training

Not only must the FSO be certified, but the cleared employees performing on classified are required to be trained as well. The training is less intensive, focusing on security responsibilities and how to be part of a security program to protect classified information. The FSO should be prepared to either teach the training or provide self-study material and capture the accomplishment in training records. Each cleared employee should participate in training.

SF-312 Briefing

SF-312 Briefing Newly cleared employees must sign an SF-312, Non Disclosure Agreement. Instead of just having them sign the box, why not give them preliminary training. What exactly is on the form and why they are signing it. Once signed, then give them the Initial

Security Briefing.

Initial Security Awareness Briefing

The initial briefing is designed to familiarize the cleared employee with the NISPOM as applied to the cleared facility. It helps ensure cleared employees know how to protect classified information and the possible penalties that they can be charged with if they contribute to unauthorized disclosure. Initial Security Awareness topics follow:

Overview of the security classification system – This information covers the levels of classification, marking, safeguarding and other tasks involved with protecting classified materials.

Employee reporting obligations – employees are required to report suspicious contacts, adverse information, security violations and incidents.

Security procedures and duties applicable to the cleared employee's job – contracts are as unique as the security programs. New employees should understand the organization specific policies as they apply to their jobs and tasks.

Threat Awareness Security Briefing Including Insider Threat-Employees learn to recognize behavior consistent with sabotage or putting classified information at risk. They also learn who and how to report the observed adverse behavior.

Counterintelligence Awareness Briefing-Employees learn to recognize behavior consistent with espionage and who and how to report the observed adverse behavior.

Overview Of The Security Classification System-How to identify and protect classified information while performing on classified contracts.

Employee Reporting Obligations And Requirements, Including Insider Threat-How and who to report adverse information.

Cybersecurity awareness training for all authorized system users-Performing on enterprise computer systems with cyber hygiene and reducing cyber risk to the CDC. This includes performing on classified information systems.

Defensive security briefing – provides information to cleared employee travel to other countries.

Annual refresher training

In addition to the initial security briefing, the FSO should provide annual refresher training to build upon the initial briefing and the on the job training. The training covers the same topics as the initial security briefing with the addition of any new changes in the national industrial security program or DSS policies since the last training event.

The changes or additional topics included in the annual refresher training should include updates to security regulations at the national level. These changes occur anytime an executive order is amended, DSS updates regulations, or any other administrative or procedural updates affecting cleared facilities and employees. Closer to home, the additional subjects could include security requirements of new classified contracts, updated security hardware, software, alarms or procedures impacting the work force.

Training should be captured by date, topic and employee name and the information kept on file for DSS review. The many methods and opportunities are limitless, but some are listed below:\

- Briefings
- Presentations
- Computer assisted learning

- Posters, flyers and banner
- Videos/Skits
- Newsletters
- Department updates

Derivative Classifier Training

As mentioned earlier, the government original classification authority makes classification decisions, contractors do not. Contractor personnel make derivative classification decisions when they incorporate, paraphrase, restate, or generate in new form, information that is already classified; then mark the newly developed material consistently with the classification markings that apply to the source information.

This training can help cleared contractors ensure that all personnel who perform duties as derivative classifiers meet the training requirements.

The NISPOM outlines requirements for derivative classification training to include… the proper application of the derivative classification principles, with an emphasis on avoiding over-classification, at least once every 2 years. Those without this training are not authorized to perform the tasks.

Insider Threat Briefing

This training program includes the NISPOM identified Insider Threat Training requirements. The NISPOM has identified the following requirements to establish an Insider Threat Program. Training should include the following topics:

- Designate an Insider Threat senior official
- Provide an Insider Threat Program / Self-certify the Implementation Plan in writing
- Establish an Insider Threat Program working group

- Provide Insider Threat training
- Monitor classified network activity
- Gather, integrate, and report relevant and credible information; detect insiders posing risk to classified information; and mitigate insider threat risk
- Conduct self-inspections of Insider Threat Program

Exit Briefings

Exit briefings – Cleared employees should be thoroughly briefed when they no longer require a clearance. A new job, loss of contract, termination, retirement and removal of access are situations where FSOs should explain the responsibility of continuing to protect the classified information.

When all individuals in the organization understand the security program and all information and tools are in place, the FSO should be able to create, implement and direct successful protection of classified information. Depending on time, resources and availability, organizations should attempt to structure security training by experience level. For example, newly cleared employees require more in depth training than veteran security clearance holders recently hired at a defense contractor organization. All newly cleared and all new cleared employees regardless of experience should receive initial refresher training before gaining access to classified information. Self study and group training presentations are available at www.redbikepublishing.com for download.

Reporting Requirements

Providing required reports to the authorized persons or agencies contributes to reducing the impact of the potential security violation, compromise or suspected compromise. Cleared employees should understand to whom and what to report. The sooner the report is issued and the more details given, the more can be done to prevent or mitigate damage to national security.

Cleared employees should be trained to report events affecting the facility security clearance or personnel security clearances. These events include threats to the security of classified information or the fact that classified information has been lost or compromised. All cleared employees should be trained how to submit reportable information internally to the FSO. Additionally, FSOs have reporting channels through the CSO and the Federal Bureau of Investigation (FBI). The quicker information gets to the proper reporting authority, the sooner it can be address and damage can be prevented or mitigated.

The FSO is charged with investigating security incidents, but getting employees to report adverse information about themselves or other employees is not easy. Security violations include: forgetting to set a combinations or alarms, losing classified items, receiving unauthorized classified information, transmitting classified material in an unauthorized manner, and etc. Each security incident should be investigated to determine whether or not loss, compromise or suspected compromise occurred. If loss, compromise or suspected compromise takes place, the FSO must notify the CSO.

FSOs should analyze and review all security incidents regardless of severity or impact. Finding root causes can provide indicators for improvements in the security system and reduction of vulnerabilities. Additionally, the CSO may ask to review any incidents and reports during the annual security inspection.

Reports to the FBI

CDCs should report to the FBI when employees become aware of any of the following events:

Espionage – Persons attempting to obtain national defense, proprietary or other sensitive information without the proper permission or clearance and need to know.

Sabotage – Persons causing damage, diversion, destruction or other activity resulting in an opponent becoming less effective.

Terrorism – These are acts to create havoc and shock in order to advance goals of ideology, money, or furtherance of political agendas.

Subversion – Acts to overthrow forms of Government authority.

Reports to the CSO

The CSO assesses other issues impacting a contractor's facility and personnel security clearances. FSOs should train cleared employee to submit information that adversely impacts the ability of a person or facility to protect classified information. More specifically, reports submitted to the CSO should include:

Adverse information – involves reports about a contractor or federal cleared employee that indicate that they may not be able to properly protect classified information. Adverse information topics include criteria found in the investigation/adjudication process:

- Allegiance to the United States
- Foreign preference
- Foreign influence
- Sexual behavior
- Personal conduct
- Financial considerations.
- Alcohol consumption
- Drug involvement
- Psychological conditions
- Criminal conduct
- Handling protected information
- Outside activities
- Use of Information Technology systems

Any activity demonstrating a violation of any of the 13 investigation criteria could define reportable adverse information. When cleared employees display any characteristics that could imply inability to protect classified material or make them vulnerable to recruitment, they should report that information.

Suspicious contacts – Any attempt by any individual to obtain unauthorized access to classified information.

Change in Status – Agencies and contractors should report any changes in status of cleared employees. These reportable changes include: name, marital status, citizenship or termination of employment.

Citizenship by naturalization – When necessary, Non-U.S. employees can be granted Limited Access Authorization.

Refusal to sign the SF 312 - Refusing the sign the SF 312 communicates lack of agreement to protect classified material or lack of training.

A change affecting the contractor facility clearance – The defense contractor is granted a clearance based in part on their ability to safeguard classified information.

Changes in storage capability – These changes include improvements or additions to the security program which raises the protection level or implement changes that deteriorate the protection level.

Inability to protect classified material – Anything preventing a cleared facility from being able to protect classified information should be reported.

Unauthorized receipt of classified material – Any classified information delivered from the cleared facility to an uncleared facility or person or classified information received without a contractual relationship should be reported.

Career Opportunities

The cleared employee job prospects are growing as fast as the US Government increases classified contracts with defense contractors. Security clearance opportunities are available at both entry and advanced level positions. When a Government entity awards classified contracts, the winning defense contractor is responsible for protecting the classified information involved.

Employees starting out in an entry level security position can experience a rewarding career. Performance, training and experience play major roles in career progression. Cleared employees are qualified to receive incredible security training provided by the CSO. Once established, a new employee can earn promotions within the organization or as hired by other defense contractors.

Security Clearance Required Jobs

There are more than 12,000 cleared Department of Defense contractor facilities. Considering that organizations can have anywhere from one to thousands of cleared employees, the amount of employees performing classified work is in the hundreds of thousands. Positions requiring security clearances include scientists working on projects to janitorial services and repair providers. Some clearances are based on actually performing classified work or just being cleared to access an area to perform repairs or cleaning services.

Even though a job may require a security clearance, an employee does not need a security clearance to apply for the job. The potential employee must only be eligible for the security clearance. Many frequently asked questions in the defense contractor field are from those who want to know how to get a security clearance so that they can apply for a job. Familiar requests include: "Can I get a security clearance in case I need to apply for another job?" Some employees in the defense industry who do not have clearances often request one just in case it is needed later. Remember that a clearance is contract and performance related; one cannot get a clearance just to apply for a job.

A job seeker's main responsibility is to find a match to a job they can do well and get the interview. The job description may require the ability to get a clearance, but uncleared people can and should apply. It is up to them to get an interview and win the job. If the potential employer finds a good match, then they will hire the employee and subsequently put in the clearance investigation request. As technology changes and homeland security needs increase, more opportunities for cleared work may arise.

Becoming a cleared contractor

Businesses and entrepreneurs considering becoming a cleared defense contractor should first become a defense contractor. Once established as a defense contractor, the new company can register and bid on government contracts, including those requiring classified work. However, getting a classified contract directly with the government is not easy. Many defense contractors have experienced success only after subcontracting with a prime cleared contractor.

Cleared Security Professionals

Each of the 12,000 facilities appoints an FSO to implement and direct a security program to protect classified information. Additionally, other CSAs (Department of Energy, Central Intelligence Agency, and Nuclear Regulatory Commission) have their own security descriptions with several more thousands of employees. In total, there are thousands of individual security opportunities in the contractor arena. The numbers increase when Government civilians and uniformed personnel are included.

The NISP provides an excellent opportunity for an employee with little experience to enter the field. For example, a veteran of the armed forces with a security clearance may find it easy to a cleared contracting or government job. Additionally, a young adult with limited work experience or skills may be able to hire with a CDC while awaiting a clearance or after getting an interim security clearance.

SUMMARY

The successful CDC should understand the incredible contribution that interaction and education lends to a winning security program designed to protect classified information. The education should be continuous, informative and increase cleared employee awareness of company policy, how to identify classified information, responsibilities to protect classified information and report required information. This begins with the cleared employee's initial security briefing and continues throughout the lifetime of their security clearance. Those working in the enterprise can be the eyes, ears and muscle extending the effectiveness of the security department.

HELPFUL WEBSITES

Training and Books on Security Clearances

Personnel and Facility Security Clearances
https://www.cdse.edu/toolkits/fsos/personnel-clearances.html
http://www.redbikepublishing.com/sf312/
http://www.redbikepublishing.com/insidersguide
https://www.cdse.edu/toolkits/fsos/facility-clearance.html

Training and Books on Protecting Classified Information

Security Awareness Posters
https://www.cdse.edu/resources/posters.html

Security Awareness Books
http://www.redbikepublishing.com/dodsecurityclearances
http://www.redbikepublishing.com/nispom/
http://www.redbikepublishing.com/selfinspectionhandbook/

Security Awareness Training
https://www.cdse.edu/toolkits/fsos/safeguarding.html
https://www.cdse.edu/toolkits/fsos/classified-visits.html
https://www.cdse.edu/toolkits/fsos/security-education.html
http://www.redbikepublishing.com/securityawareness/
http://www.redbikepublishing.com/derivative/
http://www.redbikepublishing.com/insiderthreat

ADJUDICATION EXAMPLES

THE 13 ADJUDICATIVE GUIDELINES

There are Thirteen Adjudicative Guidelines of which security clearance decisions are made. For those not aware, the security clearance process begins, maintains, and continues with background investigations, observations, and adjudication decisions. When an employee is required to perform on a classified contract, the Facility Security Officer initiates a security clearance background investigation. When an employee performs on a classified contract, their security clearance privilege is in continuous evaluation. When a cleared employee is required to continue their clearance, the FSO submits a periodic reinvestigation request.

The granting of security clearance depends on the employee demonstrating their competency to protect classified information under the 13 Adjudicative Guidelines. Security clearance investigations are more in-depth than typical employee background checks. Investigators report the results of their investigations and the government determines suitability. The results of the investigation are used to determine whether or not the subject is stable, trustworthy, reliable, of excellent character, judgment, and discretion; and of unquestioned loyalty to the United States.

These guidelines form the investigative and adjudicative foundation of which security clearance decisions are made. They continue to provide the same service during the cleared employees continuous evaluation phase and periodic reinvestigations for security clearance updates and maintenance. The subject employee should demonstrate their competency to protect classified information under the 13 Adjudicative Guidelines and continue to do so once a security clearance is granted.

At some point you may realize that your responses to the SF-86 and during investigation process that your answers may trigger red flags for one or more of the 13 criteria. Keep in mind that your responses may or may not result in the denial of a clearance. However, only the adjudicator can make that decision. No one else in the process is authorized to stop the process without the adjudicator decision.

If your security clearance is denied, you are able to provide an appeal in writing. Just be sure to be accurate and complete with your answers. If necessary, contact a lawyer who specializes in security clearance to assist with completing the form, throughout the investigation, and during adjudication.

The information below shows actual adjudication decisions based on actual events. Use the information to assist you with deciding how to fill out the form, cooperate in the investigation, tie up loose ends for historic events in your own experiences, and gathering documentation to mitigate any issues from your past.

GUIDELINE A: **Allegiance to the United States**

The applicant should demonstrate an unquestionable loyalty to the United States. If the investigation reveals that the subject belongs to or has belonged to organizations or individually supporting the overthrow of the U.S. government there is a good chance that a clearance will be denied.

Under Guideline A, decisions are based on findings of disloyal activity, not on the applications words of faithfulness. There are many ways to demonstrate questionable loyalty that outweigh verbal declarations. For example, you might think your neighbor's daily flag raising ceremony is very patriotic and you may never question their loyalty. However, your discovery of their belonging to an organization sympathetic to America's enemies may change your view. In light of their questionable associations, their reciting the Pledge of Allegiance every day is a nice gesture that is outweighed by their behavior. In a security clearance investigation, these observations may cause a denial or revocation of a security clearance; no matter how much they protest their love of America. The risk that they may compromise classified information to support their potentially true allegiance is too great.

An example of a Guideline A violation could be joining an anti-America or other hate group demonstrating desire to attack, overthrow, sabotage, or otherwise cause harm to the American government or just supporting those who do. This "joining" could be as involved as participating in activities, attending meetings, or just "liking" a social media group run by a foreign or domestic terrorist organization.

Currently, there are no security clearance decisions available on the DOHA website that are based on Guideline A violations. However, there are plenty of examples for Guidelines B and C (Foreign Influence and Foreign Preference). In other words, while Guideline A violations may be difficult to prove, the great probability of determining Guidelines B and C violations may be the next considerations to deny or revoke a security clearance. We will cover these cases in future installments.

GUIDELINE B: Foreign Influence

America is rich in international heritage and culture. We pride ourselves in our ability to expand our technology and enhance our military capability. We also recognize that much of this progress directly reflects the knowledge and technical expertise of our immigrant population. We also understand the value of American citizens living abroad who fall in love and marry spouses from their host nations. Many Americans in such situations continue to thrive in jobs requiring security clearances and many immigrants successfully obtain and maintain security clearance. However, some relationships and situations may not be favorably adjudicated. The risk to national security is just too great.

Under Guideline B, the employee bears the burden to clearly demonstrate that they are not susceptible or vulnerable to foreign influence that could lead to unauthorized theft or disclosure of classified information. Foreign influence can lead to unauthorized disclosure as the cleared employee may be coerced to provide classified information due to threat to foreign influences (friends, family, in-laws) or from foreign influences (blackmail, elicitation, favors). Where Guideline A: Allegiance to the United States, may be hard to prove Guideline B: Foreign Influence could be a paired concern. Below are real life situations of how Guideline B: can impact a security clearance decision.

Situation A: Strong Allegiance to the United States but significant Foreign Influence

In an appeal to an earlier denial of a security clearance, an applicant who emigrated to the U.S. from China states that they have demonstrated loyalty to the United States and argues that there is no reason to deny their security clearance.

However, in spite of strong demonstrations of loyalty to the U.S., they hold strong ties to relatives living in China. The applicant communicates strong sense of duty and affection to Chinese family members. These relatives could come to the attention of Chinese intelligence and become subject to pressure. This pressure could result in the applicant being coerced through family members to release sensitive data.

Situation B: Strong Allegiance to the United States but significant threat to family members

An applicant from Iraq is denied a security clearance based on civil unrest, kidnapping, and terrorism occurring in their home country and relatives living in Iraq who could be exploited. At the time of the security clearance decision, terrorist groups controlled a large portion of Iraq.

In this case, the applicant maintains contact with Iraqi family members and provides financial support. Additionally, the terrorist activity in Iraq poses a heightened risk that could lead to coercion. The applicant is vulnerable to threats to herself and family members that could bring her to a decision point between loyalty to the U.S. and her concern for her family. This could result in failing to protect sensitive information. Ties with foreign nationals are usually not a problem unless the relationship creates a security risk. The employee's relationship with family, friends, and other situations could cause them to compromise classified information. Questionable business partners, banking, investments and other business or financial involvement could cause the employee to be under obligation or duress that could present a national security risk.

Many immigrants experience great economic, academic, and professional opportunities in America. As such, they have contributed to advanced technologies and capabilities that the US has enjoyed and will continue to benefit from. However, opportunities may not always be available for security clearance jobs with cleared defense contractors. A subject's inability or unwillingness to demonstrate full allegiance to the United States of America over any other country, reduce risk of foreign influence, or demonstrate preference to the US over their own countries' of birth, the burden on national security could be too great to grant a security clearance.

GUIDELINE C: Foreign Preference

Often, Guideline C concerns appear with Guidelines A and B. Because of the close nature with Guidelines A and B, we will write this article in the same manner.

A subject under the security clearance adjudication process could have acted or be acting in ways that demonstrate preference for a foreign country. This preference could arise from being born in a foreign country, a foreign spouse, or just ideological concerns which manifest into decisions harmful to the United States. Some indications include travelling with foreign passports, serving the interests of foreign nations, or using foreign documentation to maintain foreign assets. All of which could demonstrate behavior which could lead to harm to national security.

American citizens have allowed their personal convictions and ideologies to benefit other countries; bad decisions with grave consequences. Two such spies are Jonathan Pollard and Ana Montes. Jonathan Pollard provided Top Secret information to his handler for delivery to Israel and Ana Montes provided U.S. secrets to Cuba.

Case study: Sending US Secrets to Cuba and Israel

Our first subject was born in Israel, and travels frequently to Israel with an Israeli passport to visit friends and family. He even submits his Israeli passport to his Facility Security Officer (FSO) until needed for travel. However he has not relinquished his Israeli passport because of convenience and financial costs involved with travelling on a US passport. Additionally, he demonstrated problems with Guideline: F because of continuing financial problems and tax delinquency.

While the government has clarified individuals may maintain a foreign passport, doing so for financial gain is certainly an issue.

An employee might lean toward being sympathetic to or have idealistic attitudes toward another country greater than that of the U.S. This could present a security risk.

GUIDELINE D: Sexual Behavior

It is tempting to think Guideline D only applies to sex offenders, sexual harassers, and sexual predators. It's easy to understand why a criminal may be denied a security clearance for sex crimes committed. But sexual behavior includes so much more; fetishes, prostitution, trading sex for favors, adultery, and multiple sex partners are just a few.

Sexual behavior that involves a criminal offense, indicates a personality or emotional disorder, reflects lack of judgment or discretion, or which may subject the individual to undue influence or coercion, exploitation, or duress can raise questions about an individual's reliability, trustworthiness and ability to protect classified information.

The opportunity now exists for security clearance investigators to consider an applicant's social media presence. Technical devices, social media, websites promising discreet services, and the abundance of opportunities and ease of access to many forms of sexual behavior can give a person a sense of complete privacy and no accountability. However, the same opportunities can also provide telling evidence. Discreet affairs, pornography addiction, multiple sex partners, and other behavior can be discovered using the same technology that provided the opportunity. We saw this manifested in the Ashley Madison hack.

The point is that any act committed with the intention of hiding its existence begs the question – how hard will the applicant work to keep the behavior hidden? Would they submit to blackmail, coercion, or other scheme to provide sensitive data to unauthorized persons? This point applies to any of the other guidelines to include foreign influence, alcohol abuse, foreign preference, etc.

The following cases demonstrate different manifestations of sexual behavior which have led to a denial or revocation of security clearance. Some cases involve criminal behavior while some of these clearance denials result from consensual adult decisions and do not break the law or require a court hearing.

Sexual Harassment

Making comments about another person's physical appearance, telling sexually explicit jokes, or making outright displays of a sexual nature to those who object can be considered during security clearance procedures. A judge denied a security clearance applicant who demonstrated sexual behavior of a public nature in his place of employment, The behavior is a security concern when it reflects a lack of judgment and discretion. In this case the applicant made unwanted comments and sexual advances at several companies, with some actions resulting in lawsuits. The conduct was too serious and too recent to mitigate.

Affairs, Prostitutes and "Massage Parlors"

For approximately 30 years, an applicant was involved in a variety of sexual behaviors to include continuously visiting prostitutes and receiving sexual acts in massage parlors. While the applicant attempted to rationalize these acts as legal since massage parlors are legitimate businesses, the judge deemed them of a public nature, reflecting a lack of discretion and judgment. The judge further concluded the length of applicant's sexual activities suggests a continuing problem.

Adultery – An Issue of Judgment, Blackmail

An applicant had an affair with a Japanese woman which included multiple sexual encounters. He also had sexual contact with three other citizens of foreign countries and continued to make contact with them on a regular basis. Other issues with this case fall under foreign influence and preference. Concerning the affair, he did not inform his wife about this relationship nor did he receive counseling or attempt other mitigation efforts. His clearance was denied.

Swingers and Security Clearances

Even the most open minded clearance applicants generally aren't willing to admit they regularly engage in sex acts with multiple partners. But hiding this information is one potential way of losing your security clearance. An Army Major General was removed from his sensitive position for leading a swinger's lifestyle.

Public Sex and Your Security Clearance

An applicant engaged in a public sex act; out in a park, in an open space. The applicant claimed that it was a private matter between two consenting adults. However, the applicant's privacy argument is not well-founded as the sex act did not occur in a residence or other private place such as a hotel room. If you are arrested for having sex, or being lewd in public places, your clearance could be in jeopardy. Particularly if it demonstrates a pattern of risk-taking behavior.

These are but a few of many examples of security clearance denials based on sexual behavior found in public record. There are many more not covered here where an applicant was able to successfully mitigate the issue – but it was still a red flag in the security clearance process.

GUIDELINE E: Personal conduct

The subject should demonstrate good judgment, trustworthiness, honesty, candor and a willingness to comply with rules. Any behavior otherwise may indicate irresponsibility and unsuitability to safeguard classified material.

Conduct involving questionable judgment, lack of candor, dishonesty, or unwillingness to comply with rules and regulations...Of special interest is any failure to cooperate or provide truthful and candid answers during national security investigative or adjudicative processes." Security Executive Agent Directive 4, National Security Adjudicative Guidelines. A review of security clearance adjudication decisions demonstrate that few security clearance decisions are based solely on Guideline E. They are usually paired with other guidelines such as not disclosing foreign relations, failure to repay debt, drug usage, and others. Below are but a few examples of how Guideline E has been applied to deny security clearances.

Tax Lien

Applicant was aware of a federal tax lien and a debt for reimbursement to a federal agency for overpayment. He defaulted on his payment and failed to report the information during the investigation process. As a result, he was denied a security clearance.

Stolen Valor

Applicant received a general discharge under honorable conditions for performance in the U.S. Army Reserves. However, he reported in the SF-86 that he received an honorable discharge. The applicant understood he had received a lesser of the two discharges, but claimed the more desirable discharge and lied about his military rank. Additionally, he received punishment for numerous security violations such as bringing a camera into a restricted area, failing to secure classified information, and sharing sensitive information with foreign nationals without approval. He was denied a security clearance based on his personal conduct.

Worship and Drugs

An applicant claimed that he should be able to use drugs as a matter of his religion. His drug use was determined after he had received a security clearance. The judge denied his security clearance upon reinvestigation, as the applicant's drug use occurred after having completed a clearance application and being granted a clearance. This behavior became a significant factor in evaluating his judgment and reliability.

Helping Friends

Applicant had an arrest record for battery, assault, and alcohol abuse. If that were not enough, she was also terminated for giving a free oil change to a customer. Her clearance was denied for many obvious reasons including questions about her honesty and judgment, and her ability to comply with laws, rules and regulations.

Can't Get Story Straight

This last scenario will make most supervisors, and those interested in preserving national security, grateful for the tough adjudicative process. The applicant was convicted of felony offenses three times, but marked "no" to the SF-86 question which asked whether he been charged with or convicted of any felony offense. He was also arrested on at least two other offenses, but stated "no" on the SF-86 question which asked whether he had been arrested for any offense not listed elsewhere on the SF 86 (let's bring it full circle). Same guy marks "no" to the question which asked whether he had any unpaid judgments. As such, he failed to address that a judgment was filed against him for not paying child support. Additionally, he responded "no" to questions which asked whether delinquent on any debts, which also proved to be untrue.

Just Do You

When it comes to personal conduct, applicants should demonstrate they can follow rules and regulations and make good decisions. This begins with completing the SF-86 as accurately as possible (truthfully). The SF-86 should crosswalk well with any investigation findings. If not, the gaps should be identified and mitigated. Many security clearances have been denied because the applicant was dishonest. However, many clearances were granted when the applicant was honest on the SF-86 and demonstrated during the adjudication process that they had overcome guideline issues and could be trusted with classified information.

GUIDELINE F: Financial considerations

Bad decisions affect the ability to get a security clearance. When it comes to financial mistakes, those bad decisions can linger for years to come. There are many life situations that can cause debt, that are of not fault of the debtor. Some of these situations include military deployment, relying on others to manage finances, finicky housing markets, and bad investments. Those who suffered under massive debt after the housing market burst asked, "How will my bankruptcy impact my clearance?" A quick study of security clearance decisions can provide an answer.

Some people may live above their means or fail to pay debts. They could exhibit poor self-control, lack of good judgement, or just show lack of willingness to follow to rules and regulations. This behavior raises questions about loyalty, reliability, and ability to protect classified information. Below are five specific examples of financial issues resulting in security clearance adjudication decisions.

I Just Don't Pay Taxes

An applicant's debts include failing to pay federal and state taxes and required child support. The unpaid taxes were incurred when the applicant failed to file income tax returns in a timely fashion for many years.

Though the applicant states he is trying to pay debts, he could not provide evidence of responsible behavior, nor could he provide copies of signed tax returns. Additionally, though he has agreed to repay his federal tax debt he has not provided evidence that he is in compliance with the plan. Clearance denied.

Multiple Deployments to a Combat Zone

An applicant owed thousands to the federal government for several years of unpaid taxes. Though the federal tax payments were deferred while he served, the state taxes were not. Though he claims to have paid his debt, he couldn't show proof. Additionally, he and his wife chose to pay their children's college tuition instead of the tax debt.

The applicant was denied a security clearance because of his bad decision to prioritize other payments above his obligation to the taxes he owed.

The Housing Bubble Popped

The applicant had almost a million dollars in delinquent debts that he attributed to the housing market crash. Though he owned several pieces of property they were valued lower than when he purchased them.

The applicant filed bankruptcy, but then decided to cancel and sold a house to pay off some of his debts. His debts include time share accounts, a home equity loan, and credit cards. Some of the debts were resolved through debt forgiveness and some were paid or settled for lesser amounts. However, the applicant failed to show that he had resolved two of the credit card debts.

The judge ruled against the applicant. Having debts forgiven is not the same as personally paying the debts. The applicant also showed poor judgment in many of his financial decisions. The applicant had not had effective financial counseling and there are no clear indications that his problems are under control.

Temporarily Unemployed

The applicant traces his financial difficulties to his having a disagreement with his supervisor and leaving his job, thinking that he could do better, but was not able to find good work. He got behind in his bills.

Though he eventually found work, he did not follow a plan to repay his debts and continued to acquire more debt. As a result, he failed to sufficiently mitigate the security concern and was denied a clearance.

If I Ignore It, It Will Go Away

An applicant held a significant and tardy debt to the U.S. Department of Education (USDE) for two student loans. He chose not to repay these debts, hoping that it "would just go away".

Eventually he made arrangements to start paying off this debt when he "decided it was not going to go away." He also knew that he had to get his "finances straight" because of his "job and security clearance".

Additionally, the applicant had an unpaid phone bill and ignored payments for over a year until he made arrangements to pay those debts. However, in the SF86 he responded "no" to the question, "Are you currently over 90 days delinquent on any debt(s)?" He also failed to provide a list of debts. Clearance denied.

Takeaway: Live Within Your Means and Seek Help

Though unexpected significant life and market changes can affect your financial situations, it does not always impact your security clearance. In many cases those who were in sudden significant debt due to no fault of their own, but lived within their means, attempted to pay the debt, and sought debt counseling were granted clearances. Those who ignored the debt and lived beyond their means were not granted clearances.

GUIDELINE G: Alcohol consumption

Alcohol consumption is one of the 13 adjudicative guidelines because of the possible impact of questionable judgement, failure to control impulses and the applicant's reliability and trustworthiness. These concerns are serious and could impact national security where they involve someone working with sensitive or classified information. After reviewing case studies, it's not too difficult to see the impact of alcohol use on people's lives.

Consider the following cases that demonstrate how alcohol consumption can impact security clearances. There are many more recorded, but these few will give an idea. Two cases demonstrate denial of security clearances, while one shows how the applicant adequately demonstrated mitigation and a security clearance is granted.

"I can handle it"

An applicant incurred numerous alcohol-related driving arrests. She paid fees and fines, and completed probation. However, she did not seek help in dealing with her issues with alcohol. At a later date, the applicant was involved in an accident while driving under the influence of alcohol (DUI). She was found guilty of DWI and sentenced to 180 days, paid fines and had probation.

After the last incident, she finally sought help with alcohol counseling. The counselor noted that the applicant met the diagnosis of alcohol use disorder in early remission and that her participation in therapy and continued abstinence are positive indicators. However, the applicant does not abstain from drinking, against the counselor's recommendations, and said that she feels she is in control and if there is a social event she will drink. The judge felt the applicant had not properly mitigated the concerns and denied the applicant a security clearance.

Completed some requirements

An applicant was refused a security clearance based on Guideline G, Alcohol Consumption. Later he appealed the decision stating he had adequately mitigated the behavior. The judge reiterated the facts for the appeal that demonstrated public drunkenness and driving while intoxicated. For a two-year period, the applicant actually did attend counseling for alcohol problems and was diagnosed with alcohol dependence. He reported it was in full remission. However, less than a year later he was convicted of impaired driving.

The judge supported the denial of a security clearance because of the evidence that the applicant continued to consume alcohol and become intoxicated. Though the applicant was attending counseling, he also continued to drink and drive. The applicant's behavior demonstrated that he had not done enough to mitigate the concerns.

Just need to let off some steam

Applicant took three days off work to drink as his way of dealing with stress. There was enough other evidence of alcohol use for the judge to make the finding that the applicant was abusing alcohol. One consideration is habitual or binge consumption of alcohol to the point of impaired judgment, regardless of whether the individual is diagnosed with alcohol use disorder. The security significance of the drinking episode is significant even though it did not result in an arrest or other involvement with law enforcement officials.

I'm just trying to get it right

The final applicant in this section developed a drinking problem after getting in trouble at work. He was terminated and while at home started drinking. He became dependent on alcohol and by the time he got a new job, his dependence on alcohol led to problems on his new job.

After many attempts to stop on his own, he recognized that he had a drinking problem and sought treatment. He had several relapses during treatment, but continued to be honest with counselors and his employer and continued to get help.

While he had several relapses, the judge considered the fact that he was committed to abstinence, had not consumed alcohol in two years, and is being supported by Alcoholics Anonymous and his family. In this case the judge determined the applicant had mitigated concerns and granted the request for a security clearance.

Alcohol consumption can contribute to making bad decisions that puts classified information at risk. Therefore, decisions against a security clearance may be made even if an applicant has never been charged or arrested for an alcohol related event. Abusing alcohol has proven a sufficient finding to deny a clearance. Where the applicant recognized the problem, sought treatment, and had a recent history of abstinence, the judge determined the security risk under the guideline was sufficiently mitigated.

GUIDELINE H: Drug Involvement

Drug involvement includes the abuse of illicit and legal drugs. However, a review of security clearance cases demonstrates that marijuana continues to be a concern for many applicants. New state laws, public opinion, and attitudes may make it tempting for Americans to casually use marijuana and other drugs.

Recently Colorado and other states have 'legalized' the use of marijuana and some states also allow the use of medical marijuana. Where national security is concerned, marijuana and the abuse of legal and illicit drugs for any reason is cause for denial of a security clearance.

Self Medicating

An applicant was denied a clearance for marijuana as a source of "self-medication". Applicant experienced back pain for a significant length of time and prescribed himself the benefit of marijuana to ease the pain. However, this marijuana use came to light due to an on-the-job injury and the subsequent drug test. Once busted, he went to rehab and discontinued the use. He argues that he has mitigated his earlier use with proof of rehabilitation, abstinence, and disassociation with drug-using individuals.

The judge examined all evidence and still had doubt about the applicant's ability to make good decisions. The applicant only stopped because his use was discovered during the drug test and the rehab was required and not from self-referral. The judge's findings were supported by the guidance: "Any doubt concerning personnel being considered for national security eligibility will be resolved in favor of the national security."

Culturally Savvy

Applicant stated that his marijuana use was part of his culture, even though he had been in possession of a security clearance. The applicant stated that he had decided to discontinue the use of marijuana as a personal choice and should be granted the clearance. The applicant stated that the judge should understand that though he thought he had the right to use the drug, he had decided to abstain as a deliberate effort to serve the United States. The judge disagreed, and his clearance was revoked.

"I Didn't Think it was Significant"

An applicant falsified a National Agency Questionnaire when he understated the full extent of his drug use, purchases, and sales. He falsely stated his infrequent use of marijuana only to state over the course of several interviews that he had indeed used marijuana more frequently and over a longer period of time. It wasn't until a later interview that the applicant stated he used marijuana monthly over a period of years and up until a few days prior to his final interview.

His rationale was that he did not disclose his more extensive drug because he felt they were much less significant than his other past issues. Additional considerations included use of mind altering mushrooms and the sale and purchase of drugs. The security clearance was denied.

Used it for 30 Years

An applicant used marijuana for a period of more than 30 years. He also used cocaine once in his past. He continued to use marijuana well into his work as a cleared defense contractor and stated that he would probably use it again. He has also admitted to purchasing marijuana, but had not used in six months.

The judge denied the clearance and concluded that his continuing drug abuse is clearly of present security significance.

Lots of Drugs

An applicant continued to use marijuana over an extended period of his adult life. He used the drug repeatedly and did so by stating that he ignored the fact that it was indeed illegal. Not only had he ignore the fact that marijuana was illegal and that use would disqualify him for national security jobs, but he was uncertain about future use, although he hadn't used in the past two years.

Because of his long history of marijuana use, and occasional hallucinogenic mushroom consumption, it was impossible for the judge to think his last statement to be credible. As far as mitigating the risk under Guideline H, the record is silent. He has not demonstrated the good judgment, reliability and trustworthiness required of those requesting access to the nation's secrets. The judge concluded that the applicant cannot be considered trustworthy.

Risk Mitigated

An applicant used cocaine on a number of occasions and four additional times ten years later. However, three years have passed since his last use. He states that he will never use cocaine again. Since his abstinence, he has received many recommendations from supervisors, co-workers, and friends who know him well and have vouched for his reliability, integrity, and honesty. He had received counseling for his drug use and has otherwise sufficiently demonstrated that the drug use was indeed in the past and that he would never use again. His security clearance was granted.

Just Say No

There are many reasons for drug use include cultural acceptance, lack of respect of regulations, youthful indiscretion and self-prescribed pain relief. Those who have been denied security clearances exhibit poor self-control, lack of good judgement, or just show lack of willingness to follow to rules and regulations. Drug involvement can raise questions about loyalty, reliability, and ability to protect classified information. Aside from making poor choices, abuse of prescription drugs is illegal. Inappropriate drug use leads to legal problems, personal problems and judgment issues that may make it difficult for the person to safeguard classified material.

GUIDELINE I: Psychological conditions

Security clearance decisions are favored toward protecting national security and those granted clearances should exercise sound decision making and demonstrate that they are trustworthy. Guideline I, Psychological Conditions takes into account the mental, personal, and emotional issues that can impact a person's judgement leading to impaired reliability or trustworthiness.

A diagnosis is not necessary to raise a psychological condition concern and produce a security clearance denial decision based on Guideline I. For example, a history of emotional, irresponsible, dysfunctional, violent, bizarre, and other behavior not otherwise covered under other guidelines is enough grounds to deny a clearance if not mitigated. Where an applicant has been diagnosed in the past, the Government should request consultation by qualified health care professionals.

As with other guidelines, concerns under Guideline I can be mitigated. Examples include the applicant who received treatment that controls the condition, is currently receiving counseling or treatment with a favorable prognosis, or the applicant whose previous condition is under control or in remission. Additional mitigation opportunities take into account singular events which can trigger a one-time psychological condition, such as divorce, death or other catastrophic event where the past emotional instability was a temporary condition and there is no indication of a current problem.

A review of actual security clearance cases offers only a small number of security clearance decisions based solely on Guideline I concerns. The following examples demonstrate just a few cases where security clearances were denied because of psychological conditions.

No Follow-up

An applicant had been denied a security clearance as a result of being diagnosed as bipolar and other issues under other Guidelines (drug and alcohol dependence). While he successfully mitigated some issues, he did not mitigate his bipolar diagnosis. He simply did not pursue a new diagnosis or get documentation to mitigate concerns under Guideline I. While he had presented character references for trustworthiness, without the proper follow-up from with a qualified medical professional, his clearance request was denied.

Symptoms Continue

An applicant had been diagnosed with bipolar disorder and paranoid schizophrenia. Since then, they have continued to receive treatment. During the clearance process, Defense Office of Hearings and Appeals (DOHA) requested that a mental health professional perform a psychological evaluation. The psychologist also diagnosed the applicant with a psychotic and schizo-affective disorder. The psychologist further expressed the opinion that the applicant could continue to experience symptoms that could put classified information at risk and a clearance was denied.

Likely to Relapse

An applicant had been diagnosed with schizophrenia. During the security clearance process, DOHA requested an evaluation from a qualified mental health professional. The psychiatric expert also diagnosed schizophrenia but no current psychological problems and therefore found the mental condition to be in remission. However, the expert did determine that the applicant is still likely to have a future relapse. The applicant's thought process, if relapse occurred, could put classified information at risk.

In comparison with other security clearance issues, there were but a few cases over a 10 year period where Guideline I applied. Where applicants have received a past psychological condition diagnosis, the government requested consultation by qualified health care professionals. In these cases, the mitigations were not strong enough to reduce risk enough to grant security clearances.

Persons suffering under mental, personality and emotional challenges could be unable to perform in normal social or work environments. This could also affect their judgment and suitability for a clearance. Emotional, mental and personality disorders can cause a person to make bad decisions concerning classified information or make them incapable of protecting classified information.

GUIDELINE J: Criminal conduct

Criminal activity creates doubt about a person's judgment, reliability and trustworthiness. Criminal behavior is an indicator of whether or not an applicant will follow laws, rules and regulations. This is a critical concern where cleared employees are expected to comply with NISPOM guidance, rules, and laws as they discharge their duties and protect classified information. In fact, an applicant does not even have to be charged, prosecuted, or convicted to cause a security clearance denial.

The following cases demonstrate how applicants clearly violated laws and directives. Their security clearances were denied because their criminal behavior created doubt about their ability to protect classified information.

I Made You Say Underwear

For some reason, the applicant decided to undress and parade around in his underwear. After undressing in a department store's dressing room, the applicant left the room in only his underwear four times before security approached him. Police were called and the applicant was issued a citation.

The applicant's clearance was denied and on appeal, the applicant stated that the employee misunderstood what he was doing and that the judge had not accounted for "the complexity of human behavior."

However, the appeal judge upheld the original decision. The judge observed that the applicant did not provide any evidence or statements from friends or family that support the applicant's statements, or that would mitigate his actions. In absence of character references and evidence of innocence or habilitation, the clearance remains denied.

Can you imagine using such rationale as a reason to release classified information in an unauthorized manner? "Well Your Honor, I'm a complex person and you should not question my decision to provide this sensitive information to our foreign guests."

Only Gets DUI's When He Drinks

An applicant has had three arrests and convictions for DUI over the course of five years. As a result, the applicant attended court ordered counseling and treatment. The clinician did not give the applicant a diagnosis nor recommend substance abuse treatment. The applicant stopped drinking after the first two DUI incidents, but started again before the third. He now drinks a few times per month and has had no further incidents in the past two years.

The judge ruled in favor of denying a security clearance. Though the applicant has provided evidence of a great work history, he has not had enough time to demonstrate a pattern of responsible drinking and provide adequate mitigation.

Though the judge seemed to have ruled correctly, the applicant states that he rarely drank and that the judge ruled against him in error. The applicant stated he seldom drank.

Using his rationale, it was only when he drank that he actually received DUIs. It would be safe to assume that by the similar rationale, the only time classified information is at risk is when an applicant has access to it. In this case, the judge wasn't willing to take that chance.

Liar Liar

An applicant was arrested and pled guilty to assault after badly beating his wife. He later attended anger management counseling. However, based on his former wife's written statements, this was not a one-time incident. He physically abused her on many occasions.

In spite of the former spouse's written statements, the applicant falsified his own sworn statement by saying that he had not physically abused his wife other than the one time incident. Additionally, he offered little in the way of mitigation, and the clearance was denied.

Using this rationale, a cleared employee could falsify end of day security checks. He could just sit at his desk and check off all the blocks without even walking around and inspecting the areas of concern.

Uninformed Decision

An applicant decided not to file his tax return and missed many deadlines to file thereafter. He failed meet one extension deadline after the next. However, one day he decided he was going to file and he owned up to it. When he came up for a security clearance investigation, Guideline J concerns arose.

The administrative judge at the time determined that the applicant mitigated the Guideline J consideration simply by finally filing the tax return. However, the government appealed because adjudication had not been met as … "The person did not voluntarily commit the act and/or the factors leading to the violation are not likely to recur".

The applicant purposefully missed all deadlines until he finally filed, when he finally got to it. There is no reason to indicate that this behavior may not occur at a later date. Additionally, the applicant claimed to believe he owed no taxes. However, he did indeed still owe back taxes.

Could you imagine how this could put classified information at risk? Using this rationale, a cleared worker could decide to ignore National Industrial Security Program Operating Manual (NISPOM) guidance and not mark classified material properly. He could continue to put unmarked classified information at risk until he was good and ready to mark it properly and lock it in a secure container. As long as he eventually got to it, his good intention is all that counts.

Guideline J concerns are appropriate for evaluating security clearance requests. Where investigations uncover violations of laws, regulations and rules, the adjudicators have a duty to understand whether or not the behavior has been mitigated. Criminal activity, whether prosecuted or not, could be an indicator that an applicant could put national security in jeopardy.

GUIDELINE K: Handling protected information

Person's who cannot protect privacy, physical inventory or other privileged information may have problems protecting classified material. Employees who have demonstrated a destain or willingness to violate security policy could prove a risk to national security.

Applicants for security clearance must demonstrate that they can protect sensitive information. Under Guideline K, "deliberate or negligent failure to comply with rules and regulations for protecting classified or other sensitive information raises doubt about an individual's trustworthiness, judgment, reliability, or willingness and ability to safeguard such information, and is a serious security concern." Any history of allowing unauthorized access, forgetting to enforce security rules, or loaning out passwords will definitely raise red flags and call trustworthiness into question. Review the following cases and see if you can identify the Guideline K issues.

You're Just Trying to Catch Me

A clearance holder brought a camera into a restricted area against security rules. Additionally he committed many other security violations to include discussing sensitive information with unauthorized non-U.S. persons in an unauthorized area, left foreign nationals unattended with a classified workstation, and did not store classified hard drives. He was formally disciplined and removed from his place of employment due to continuous disregard of security procedures.

These are not only security violations, but due to the foreign national and non-U.S. person aspect, the individual, his company, and fellow employees are at risk of export licensing and International Traffic In Arms Regulation violations.

During the hearing, he failed to produce any mitigating circumstances, provide explanation, or offer character witness statements. He did state, however, that the charges were lies spread by persons who did not like him and were "out to get [him]."

COMSEC and Higher Than SECRET

Some classified information requires additional protection because of the very nature of its existence; Communications Security (COMSEC) information is one example. Those with access to COMSEC are required to attend additional training and sign documents prior to possession of COMSEC material.

While accessing COMSEC information, an individual failed to practice security requirements on many occasions. These violations include failing to close and lock a COMSEC security container or secure a COMSEC vault door, leaving classified information in an unsecure area, and a few other incidents that put COMSEC at risk.

The applicant did provide mitigations, to include character witnesses, work accomplishments, and how she is a stellar performer. However, the mitigations did not address the security violation concerns. Though the incident happened in the past, the judge still had questions and doubts about her ability to protect classified information and denied the clearance.

Don't Give Out Your Passwords; Seriously...Don't

A Federal Information System is provided to a Facility Security Officers (FSO) use to maintain facility and personnel clearances and contains sensitive information. DCSA requires users to hold a security clearance and trains them to never share their usernames and passwords.

In this case, while the individual had received training from the Defense Security Service, he knowingly provided his username and password and granted unauthorized access to sensitive information. He provided his username and password to an uncleared employee for almost two years, allowing him to delegate FSO and system responsibilities. Because of the potential risk to sensitive and classified information and the frequency and length of time the violations occurred, the violations were not mitigated and the judge denied the applicant's security clearance.

I Only Spied Because I was Cheating

A married applicant gained access to his girlfriend's e-mail without permission or authorization. This included a classified e-mail account that contained information of which he did not have need to know. This violates Guideline K as "inappropriate efforts to obtain or view classified or other protected information outside one's need-to-know". Additionally, as a privileged information system user, he took advantage of his position to gain information for his own personal use and did not practice the requirement to accountable for his actions on an information system.

The applicant did however provide mitigation, to include admitting to his wife that he had had an affair, reconciling with his wife and demonstrating a passage of time since the events occurred (four years).

Additional mitigations included the attendance of many security trainings, and a demonstration of his excellent attitude toward security rules. The judge ruled that the security incidents are "unlikely to recur and does not cast doubt on the individual's reliability, trustworthiness, or good judgment," and that "the individual responded favorably to counseling or remedial security training and now demonstrates a positive attitude toward the discharge of security responsibilities,". The seriousness of the applicant's conduct was outweighed by the presence of rehabilitation and the amount of time elapsed since its occurrence

The ability to demonstrate trustworthiness and proclivity to protection classified and protected information is often based on history. Any red flags or shortfalls with obeying rules and regulations set for protecting protected data surely must be mitigated. In the above cases only one was mitigated and the clearance granted. This decision was based on the work that the applicant spent to rehabilitate himself and demonstrate that his violations were history, and that his future included a focused security attitude.

GUIDELINE L: Outside activities

Sometimes work or activities conflict with the ability to maintain a security clearance. This involvement with outside activities also includes volunteer or non-profit work.

Outside activities (Guideline L of the adjudicative criteria) refers to jobs or relationships occurring outside of the United States and involving relationships with foreign countries, persons and businesses. With the internet, social media, and global connectivity, there are many opportunities to meet other like-minded business people. The world is getting smaller, and opportunities to connect are increasing. Forming businesses with foreign people and companies can create new jobs, products, and services. These opportunities come with a cost to those who might seek a government security clearance. Let's look at a few examples:

Earning Half of Your Income From a Foreign Company

An applicant is the president and CEO of a company incorporated in Singapore. Key management employees and decision makers are foreign citizens and almost half of his income is from the company. He spends time overseas, with foreign citizens, and other foreign companies related to his business.

His ability to safeguard classified and sensitive information could be influenced by his business interests, foreign relationships, or financial portfolio. Pressure from his outside activities could cause him to disclose classified or sensitive information to unauthorized persons through coercion or exploitation. The applicant was denied a security clearance in favor of the national security. Remember, the government will always err on the side of protecting its own interests. When a person has more than a half-interest and significant relationships in a foreign country, there is cause for concern.

Hail Britannia

The applicant is the president of an American subsidiary of a British-based company that does business with the Department of Defense. Prior to the promotion, he was an employee at the same foreign company. He has a substantial financial stake with the company by virtue of his high valued stock. Because of his employment in the foreign organization and serving as a representative of the foreign country, his clearance was denied. His high position in the company, share of stocks, and possible relationships with foreign partners could cause him to be vulnerable to coercion or exploitation.

Ending the Relationship

An applicant worked as vice president of business development for a wholly-owned subsidiary of an Israeli company. In his position, he marketed computer hardware and software to U.S. companies. He was hired for the job after meeting the owner at a trade show, but had very infrequent interaction with the owner.

The applicant has not worked for the company in a few years. Also he no longer has ties with the company neither by positions, finances, relationships, or shares. His relationship and interaction with his former employer and employees is infrequent, if ever. The applicant has mitigated concerns raised by Guideline L by completely separation himself from the business. This demonstrated separation has greatly reduced the likelihood of any potential security incident and therefore he was granted a security clearance.

Outside activities where U.S. persons enjoy foreign positions, relationships, and financial benefits can be rewarding, but do come with a cost. Security clearance applicants should demonstrate that they are not bringing additional risk to classified or sensitive information through their outside activities. The concern for Guideline L is that certain types of outside employment or activities is a security concern if it poses a conflict of interest with an individual's security responsibilities, and could create an increased risk of unauthorized disclosure of classified or sensitive information. Often, the only way to mitigate the potential concern is by severing ties with those foreign entities, particularly financial ones.

GUIDELINE M: Use Of Information Technology

Remember the old saying? "Rank has its privilege"? It's not always prudent to assume certain privileges just because you have means and intent. It's not safe to assume just because you have access to government Information Technology (IT) systems as a manager or system administrator, for example, that you have the authority to do so anytime and for any reason. Use of government IT systems takes into consideration how an applicant has used technology on the job. Viewing pornography, working non-mission related tasks, hiding evidence, and harassing fellow employees while using employer computers are some indicators that an applicant could bring risk to sensitive information residing on information technology.

Cleared employees must demonstrate the ability to follow rules and regulations. This is especially critical as more and more sensitive information resides on computers. Gaining unauthorized access, downloading malware, manipulating data, or otherwise misusing information technology could increase risk to sensitive and classified information. An applicant's history and pattern of use can provide indicators of their ability to protect what resides on information systems. The following are case studies where Guideline M concerns were either mitigated or clearance was denied:

Cyber Powered Sex Addict

An applicant installed an e-mail program on the company's computer to allow him to access anonymous e-mail accounts. He also logged onto pornographic sites, downloaded pornographic materials, wrote and posted 30 sexually explicit stories, doctored a photograph of a female former coworker in a sexually explicit manner and posted it, sought sexual partners and engaged in sexual activity as a result of people answering the posted requests. The applicant was eventually fired for the activity.

The applicant did seek help and engaged in group therapy including a sexual compulsive addicts' group. Sponsors, group participants and counselors made statements that the applicant was indeed recovering and demonstrates remorse for his activities. Both he and his wife are continuing to get marriage counseling.

The judge ruled favorably in that the applicant mitigated the risk to national security for the concern Use of Information Systems. However, he was not able to mitigate other concerns such as those that arose from his Personal Conduct and Sexual Behavior.

I Was Going to Return Them

After a female employee accused him of sexual harassment, the applicant decided to take matters into his own hands. His plan was to temporarily hide incriminating e-mail so that his coworkers would not find the files. The applicant followed through and took advantage of his position to move the implicating e-mail to a separate location, with the intent of moving them back.

Unfortunately for him, he was unable to restore the files following a software upgrade. The messages were lost and could not be restored. His deeds were discovered, and Guideline M concerns had to be addressed in a hearing.

Surprisingly, the judge ruled in favor of the applicant. The judge determined that the applicant did not intend to delete the files. Government counsel was concerned that he was granted a security clearance although he gained authorized access to her computer to get rid of evidence.

Had I Known You Were Looking...

An applicant used his government computer to download pornography; clearly violating policies, rules, and regulations to misuse his computer. Further, when interviewed by Defense Security Services (DSS), he lied about the incident.

He responded in the hearing the he was very sorry and that he did not mean to break rules. He also stated that had he known that the pornographic files existed on his computer, he would not have lied about accessing the porn. He also offered that the incident happened a few years prior and that he has been given increasing responsibilities and positions of trust since then.

Unfortunately, saying sorry is not enough. While a good first step, it does not mitigate the activity. Additionally, whether records of adverse behavior exist, he has no excuse for falsifying his statement to DSS. As a result, his clearance was denied.

Because of the increasing reliance on information systems, a cleared employee must be able to demonstrate that they can be trusted to not abuse privileges, information systems, and responsibilities. Past performance that demonstrates breaking information system policies, procedures, rules and regulations indicate potential risk to information residing on the systems. Employees who use computers as intended and only for authorized and work-related projects should have no problems demonstrating compliance with Guideline M.

Breaking company policy concerning the use of technology and computer systems can indicate lack of obedience to rules and regulations. Inappropriate use of the internet, computers, fax machines, alarms and networks could indicate that an employee cannot adequately protect classified systems.

Summary

Subjects who fall under any of the above criteria will not automatically be denied a security clearance. There are situations where people have committed crimes or used drugs, but have had clearances awarded because of corrective behavior or other mitigating circumstances. They may have sought professional counseling or other types of treatment. Employees who had abused alcohol may have attended rehabilitation. Some may have demonstrated disqualifying behavior because at the time they suffered emotional problems from incidents such as a death or divorce, or the indicated incidences had transpired way back in their personal histories. When considering a person for a clearance, the adjudicator will assess each case based on the whole person concept.

The applicant can do some things to speed up the security clearance process and help mitigate any of the above issues. Primarily, they should gather as much information and related records as available. It is important for the applicant to fill out the security clearance request information accurately and completely and provide any supporting documents. The adjudicator will only be able to rely on the information provided in the investigation and the applicant's SF 86. Willful or voluntary disclosure of adverse information can prove helpful during the adjudicative process.

APPENDIX

Typically when a new employee is hired to perform on a classified contract, the Facility Security Officer (FSO) enters them into the government's information system. If the employee already has an active security clearance, then the action is administrative; just a transfer. Where a new employee does not have a security clearance, the FSO will initiate the investigation request.

The applicant completes and submits the SF-86 with the security officer's assistance and the investigation begins. Next, the adjudicators apply the "whole person" concept to determine suitability and make a security clearance decision.

The applicant has some control over the timeliness of the application and duration of investigation when they put in the effort to prepare ahead of time with all the references necessary to answer questions accurately and completely. Additionally they can also gather references that may help the adjudicators understand whether or not any derogatory information can be overcome. The majority of questions seek answers necessary to make a determination based on the 13 Adjudicative Guidelines. Any answers to the questions indicating a risk should be explained in as much detail as possible. Where there is doubt or question, the applicant should err on the side of over explaining instead of under explaining answers. Aside from artifacts explaining situations, the applicant may seek legal advice to assist in completing the document.

My independent research into whether "unpardonable activity" exists or to answer any questions asking what behavior would always disqualify anyone for a security clearance leads me to answer that it depends on the situation and how the applicant demonstrates a turn from that behavior. However, some applicant behavior that has contributed to security clearance denials include:

• A cavalier attitude about their behavior. In other words the attitude of "take me as I am and I won't change for you."

• Lying on the application. These lies include excluding crucial information as well as pretending it never happened.

• The incident in question occurred within the past 12 months. Aside from circumstances leading to an incident in question, recency is a big issue; the more recent the incident, the more difficult it is to mitigate.

If an applicant is indeed concerned that past events may lead to the denial of a security clearance, they should provide as much information as possible explaining or demonstrating that the events are in the past, will not be repeated, completely overcome with rehabilitation, and successfully an non-issue as far as motivation to do it again, ability to be coerced or exploited, or a temptation to do again.

The adjudicators consider the following as they try to make a decision as to whether or not the applicant will be a national security risk. They make security clearance decisions based on interest to national security. Consequently, the applicant is required to demonstrate they are not a threat to national security and should provide artifacts demonstrating that though they may have been a risk to national security at one point, that risk has been mitigated.

Let's consider the following from the adjudicator's point of view. Each of the 9 points can be applied to each of the 13 Adjudicative topics from foreign influence to computer usage. For the sake of this writing, let's apply to drug usage specifically. The reader can expand the application to whichever adjudicative topic(s) they need to cover.

1. the nature, extent, and seriousness of the conduct. The adjudicator would want to know what type of drugs were being used, and the

amount of drugs being used at each occurrence.

2. the circumstances surrounding the conduct, to include knowledgeable participation. This is where you can explain why you used drugs. Was it a one-time use after coercion from a peer group, or part of a religious practice? Was it a bad decision based on a drunken event or just something you wanted to do? The point is to paint a picture of the motivation behind the drug use so that later you can explain whether or not the circumstances still apply.

3. the frequency and recency of the conduct. Here is where the adjudicator views how often the drug use occurred and when the last time drugs was used. If enough time has passed since the last drug use (a year or more) the drug use risk could be mitigated.

4. the individual's age and maturity at the time of the conduct. This again points to reasons behind the drug use. If it occurred many years previously and while the applicant was younger and the result of a few bad decisions while in school, then it could be mitigated.

5. the extent to which participation is voluntary. This extend could cover being a participant during a group experiment to actually supplying drugs to the party goers. The adjudicator will want to have a good understanding of the behavior that led to drug usage contrasted with your current potential to reengage.

6. the presence or absence of rehabilitation and other permanent behavioral changes. Completing a rehabilitation program demonstrates a motivation toward positive change. Voluntary rehabilitation and completion is a positive endeavor. Quitting rehabilitation is going to be a concern. If you attended rehabilitation, you may want to explain the circumstances to include counselors' notes, certificates, and letters of recommendation or other artifacts that support or demonstrate a permanent change in attitude or behavior.

7. the motivation for the conduct. This is a direct request for

information. The adjudicator much understand the mental attitude behind the behavior. Was the attitude cavalier, did it reflect entitlement, or was it a weak moment never to be repeated. The thought is that past motivation could reoccur if not mitigated. An applicant could provide statements from friends, co-workers, contemporaries or other influential people supporting a character change. This will help the adjudicator visualize a change in motivation or attitude.

8.   the potential for pressure, coercion, exploitation, or duress. If the applicant has an attitude in favor of drug use, a feeling of entitlement to use drugs, or has a drug positive ideal, this could be a huge factor. However, statement, letters of recommendation, or completion of rehabilitation programs could prove to mitigate this potential in the eyes of the adjudicator.

9.   the likelihood of continuation or recurrence. The adjudicator has to put all 8 points to the test. Once they consider the whole person concept, they've got to rule in favor of national security on this one. If the likelihood of recurrence or continuation exists, the clearance will be denied.

 In summary, regarding each of the 13 Adjudicative Criteria, the applicant should gather all information available to explain the behavior that could cause a denial of a security clearance. Below is a list of supporting evidence and artifacts that could be used to reduce the risk of a security clearance denial. We are listing general guidelines that span all 13 Adjudicative topics. Use all appropriate based on you your situation. The following is not a complete list, but should get the applicant to think about what documents, resources, and artifacts they should provide in response to the SF-86 application.

Criteria	Artifact	Mitigations
Guideline A: Allegiance to the United States	• Proof of US Citizenship • Proof of Non-US Citizenship • Marriage Certificate • Documentation identifying foreign relationships and dealings • Business documents identifying foreign business • Financial statements identifying foreign investments	• Memorandum expressing allegiance to the United States • Character references (signed statements) • Statement proving dissolution of questionable memberships • Proof of foreign business or financial dissolution or mitigation
U.S. Guideline B: Foreign Influence	• Proof of US Citizenship • Proof of Non-US Citizenship • Birth Certificate • Marriage Certificate • Business documents • Financial statements	• Memorandum expressing allegiance to the United States • Character references (signed statements) • Statement proving dissolution of questionable memberships • Proof of foreign business or financial dissolution or mitigation • Proof of dissolution of foreign influence
Guideline C: Foreign Preference	• Proof of US Citizenship • Proof of Non-US Citizenship • Birth Certificate • Marriage Certificate • Business documents • Financial statements	• Memorandum expressing allegiance to the United States • Character references (signed statements) • Statement proving dissolution of questionable memberships • Proof of foreign business or financial dissolution or mitigation
Guideline D: Sexual Behavior	• Formal complaint • Court records • Arrest record • Counseling records	• Character statements by references • Proof of successful counseling
Guideline E: Personal Conduct	• Formal complaint • Court records • Arrest record • Statements by references	• Character statements by references • Proof of successful counseling
Guideline F: Financial Considerations	• Financial statements • Missed Payment • Mortgage statements	• Debt consolidation • Debt forgiveness • Final payment • Statement from creditors
Guideline G: Alcohol Consumption	• Alcohol related police reports (DUI, Arrests, etc.) • Alcohol related employee reports (Letters of termination, referrals to counseling)	• Character statements by references • Proof of successful counseling
Guideline H: Drug Involvement	• Arrest records • Court records • Failed urinalysis	• Character statements by references • Proof of successful counseling
Guideline I: Psychological Conditions	• Doctor's diagnosis • Police reports • Employer disciplinary action	• Character statements by references • Proof of successful counseling

Guideline J: Criminal Conduct	• *Police reports* • *Police reports* • *Employer disciplinary action* •	• *Character statements by references* • *Proof of successful counseling*
Guideline K: Handling Protected Information	• Employer disciplinary action • Security incident reports • Loss of security clearance	• Character statements by references • Completion of training
Guideline L: Outside Activities	• Documentation identifying foreign relationships and dealings • Business documents identifying foreign business • Financial statements identifying foreign investments	• Memorandum expressing allegiance to the United States • Character references (signed statements) • Statement proving dissolution of questionable memberships • Proof of foreign business or financial dissolution or mitigation
Guideline M: Use of Information Technology	• Police reports • Employer disciplinary action	• Character statements by references • Completion of training

ABOUT THE AUTHOR

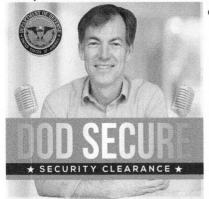

Jeffrey W. Bennett ISP, ISOC, SAPPC, SFPC is a security expert with experience in the Army, U.S. Government and as a Facility Security Officer (FSO). He holds ISP certificate number 117. Jeff developed this study manual to help motivate his peers and offer them an opportunity to take practice tests.

Jeff is enthusiastic about protecting our nation's secrets. He believes that integrity, influence and credibility are paramount qualities required of security professionals. His primary goal is to show security specialists how to bring about security awareness, build influence within the organization and to make a difference where they work.

He speaks, writes and provides products to help professionals better protect sensitive and classified information. Red Bike Publishing's Unofficial Study Guide for: *ISP Certification-The Industrial Security Professional* l provides security education and helps security specialists earn their certification. Additionally, Jeff is the author of *How to Win U.S. Government Contracts and Classified Work, Insider's Guide to Security Clearances, Get Rich in a Niche-Insider's Guide to Self Publishing* and several novels. Contact jeff editor@redbikepublishing. com

Hear Jeff's Podcast at https://www.redbikepublising.com/dodsecure

Join NISPOM and ISP Cert training at https://bennettinstitute.com

Red Bike Publishing

Our company is registered as a government contractor company with the CCR and VetBiz (DUNS 826859691). Specifically we are a service disabled veteran owned small business. Red Bike Publishing provides high quality books and training @ www.redbikepublishing.com

Publishing
Get Rich in a Niche-The Insider's Guide to Self-Publishing in a Specialized Industry ISBN: 978-1-936800-04-9

Other Topics
1. *2000 Miles On Wisdom* ISBN: 978-1-936800-20-9
2. *Around the Corner-Reflections on American Wars, Violence, Terrorism, and Hope* ISBN: 978-1-936800-22-3
3. *Next in Line Please* ISBN: 978-1-936800-15-5
4. *Rainy Street Stories-Reflections on Secret Wars, Espionage and Terrorism* ISBN: 978-1-936800-10-0

Novels
Commitment-A Novel ASIN: B0057U3GLS
Devoted ASIN: B015HTZW1K

National Security
1. *How to Win U.S. Government Contracts and Classified Work* ISBN 978-1-936800-26-1
2. *ISP Certification-The Industrial Security Professional Exam Manual* ISBN: 978-0-981620-60-2
3. *National Industrial Security Program Operating Manual (NISPOM)* ISBN: 978-0-98162060-85-7
4. *International Traffic in Arms Regulation (ITAR)* ISBN: 978-0-9816-28-8

A special word of thanks and a favor to ask

Thank You For Reading Insider's Guide to Security Clearances. I really hope you find it helpful.

I really would really love to hear your feedback and your input would help to make the next version of this book and my future books better.

Please leave me a helpful review on Amazon letting me know what you thought of the book.

I would also ask that you let a friend know about our book as well.

Thanks so much and best of success to you!!

Jeffrey W. Bennett.

Like us on Facebook. Our page is DoD Security @ https://www.facebook.com/dodsecure

If you want more information about Red Bike Publishing, check out our video.
http://www.redbikepublishing.com/security/

Made in the USA
Monee, IL
11 May 2022

96222006R00083